Sarah Ockwell-Smith is the mother of four children. She has a BSc in Psychology and worked for several years in pharmaceutical research and development. Following the birth of her first child, Sarah re-trained as an antenatal teacher and birth and postnatal doula. She has also undertaken training in hypnotherapy and psychotherapy. Sarah specialises in gentle parenting methods and is co-founder of the Gentle Parenting website www.gentleparenting.co.uk.

Sarah is the author of thirteen other parenting books: *BabyCalm, ToddlerCalm, The Gentle Sleep Book, The Gentle Parenting Book, Why Your Baby's Sleep Matters, The Gentle Discipline Book, The Gentle Potty Training Book, The Gentle Eating Book, The Second Baby Book, The Starting School Book, Between, How to Be a Calm Parent* and *Beginnings*. She frequently writes for magazines and newspapers, and is often called upon as a parenting expert for national television and radio.

SARAH OCKWELL-SMITH

Because I Said So!

Why society is childist
and how breaking the cycle of
discrimination towards children
can change the world

PIATKUS

PIATKUS

First published in Great Britain in 2023 by Piatkus

1 3 5 7 9 10 8 6 4 2

Copyright © Sarah Ockwell-Smith 2023
The moral right of the author has been asserted.

A CIP catalogue record for this book
is available from the British Library.

ISBN: 978-0-349-43646-3

Typeset in Stone Serif by M Rules

Printed and bound in Great Britain by
Clays Ltd, Elcograf S.p.A.

Papers used by Piatkus are from well-managed forests
and other responsible sources.

Piatkus
An imprint of
Little, Brown Book Group
Carmelite House
50 Victoria Embankment
London EC4Y 0DZ

An Hachette UK Company
www.hachette.co.uk

www.littlebrown.co.uk

Contents

What is Childism?

'Because I said so!'

How many times did you hear this phrase from your parents or carers when you were a child, having dared to question the wisdom of adult authority? I'd wager quite a lot. Maybe you were frequently ordered to 'just do as you're told!'? Or perhaps you remember hearing a countdown in stern tones: 'three ... two ... one'? Many of us will recall being scared into submission before the countdown was complete; others will remember being on the receiving end of a swift slap across the backs of our legs, or being dragged to sit in another room, alone, to think about our so-called disobedience and disrespect just a few moments after hearing the word 'zero'.

I have been working with parents, as an educator and coach, for the last two decades. When I ask them to remember times of disobedience from their own childhoods, the exercise is always met with chuckles, fond head shaking and misty-eyed reminiscence of good times, as they recollect a parent's or carer's words and actions. They believe that they deserved the so-called discipline. They tell me they were 'a right handful' or 'a naughty child'. They smile as they say, 'Ah, but it never did me any harm!'

They are wrong.

This mistreatment of children – the most vulnerable members of society – is neither funny nor just. The trouble is, it is ingrained into our society; it has become acceptable, advisable, even. We celebrate leaving babies to cry alone at night in their cribs in the name of sleep training and 'teaching them to self-soothe', even though self-soothing at such a young age is developmentally impossible. We live in a world where people think nothing of isolating a child from their family and peers, shaming them, punishing them, and often reducing them to tears, in the name of entertainment for television shows and social media clips, all without the child's consent. Our governments seem hell-bent on making life as difficult as possible for families, and particularly for children, the only constituents who don't get a say in their futures. And we do all of this on the back of historical male child-care experts, who gave advice over a century ago, their theories buried deep in patriarchal beliefs.

We rarely question our thoughts, words and actions, and if we do, we brush aside any concerns on the basis that we think we turned out OK. Sometimes, when an argument seems sound and logic cannot be easily used to refute it, the messenger is ridiculed as a 'woke snowflake', 'liberal lefty' or worse. These personal attacks should be called out for their shaky philosophical basis, yet they are the mainstay of mainstream media today – and many people who follow it. We blindly perpetuate the discrimination of children and ridicule and ostracise those who attempt to stand up for them, in a pattern that continues from generation to generation.

What is childism?

Childism is no different from any other 'ism' – racism, sexism, ageism, heterosexism (more commonly known as homophobia) and ableism. It simply refers to the discrimination of children in our society. You could argue that childism is a form of ageism, since ageism is usually defined as being treated unfairly, or discriminated against, because of age. The term ageism, however, is usually used to refer to the middle-aged and elderly in society and doesn't address the unique barriers, discrimination and mistreatment faced by the young. Children are often believed to be spoiled rotten, showered with constant love, attention and money; therefore they cannot be discriminated against or poorly treated in the same way as older members of society.

The more books I write about parenting and childcare (this is my fourteenth), the more I realise that the answers to the questions I am most frequently asked (usually starting with 'How do I get my child to . . .') should not be about changing the behaviour of children but, rather, about changing our beliefs and actions as adults. Because if adults truly understood childism and vowed to be better, and *do* better, as is the case with other 'isms', then the way we treat children would be radically different.

You may be surprised to learn that, as a mother of four and a so-called parenting expert, I am not a 'baby person' and I don't have a natural bond with children. In fact, aside from my own, I am often awkward around them, which is embarrassing when I chat with parents after a book signing, talk or workshop and a smiling baby is foisted into my arms for a quick photo. Given this lack of affinity with babies and children, I'm often asked why I do what I do? Why am I so doggedly determined to change the way children are viewed and treated? The truth is that my real passion is fighting injustice. I don't believe that children are treated fairly by society and yet they are the last discriminated group that we talk about. Children are discriminated against by adults from all walks of life – from parents and government officials to those who work in the education system: the very adults who are meant to protect and advocate for them. This needs to change.

What is the purpose of this book?

My aim with this book is threefold: first, to help you to understand your past and the childism you faced. To help you to see that the way you were treated as a child was often unjust and unfair and to reflect on whether this childist treatment has shaped your beliefs and behaviours. Next, I hope to help you consider the present and to see the extent of childism in society today, whether to help you to change the way you are with your children (or the children in your care) or perhaps, instead, to reinforce the approach you are already taking. Finally, we will look to the future and changes – some small, some big – that could transform the way our society treats children, with lasting positive effects for future generations.

Who is this book for?

In short, it's for everyone. We have all been affected by childism because we have all been children. Some will be drawn to this book for information to help them with parenting their own children, others will find the book validating and useful to help with understanding themselves and their own upbringings. I have also written the book with professionals in mind, including childcare workers, teachers, government employees and medical professionals who work with children and their carers. This is a book for every adult who cares about our world and its future.

While much of the book will focus on childism in the early years, with babies and toddlers, we will also look at how discrimination impacts older children – because childism doesn't stop as they get older, it just changes. To fully grasp the extent of childism in society today, though, we need to understand the roots of discrimination at the very beginning of childhood. The views and actions of adults towards infants shape the relationships and treatment of children as they grow into tweens, teens and young adults. So, regardless of whether you have, or care for, a one-year-old, a ten-year-old or a seventeen-year-old, we must start at the very beginning to fully understand how children, whatever their age, are affected today.

What you will find in this book

In the following ten chapters, we will consider how childism impacts different areas of a child's life and highlight the discrimination. While this book is intended to raise awareness of an issue that has been ignored and avoided for far too long, it is also a rallying call to arms. Knowing about childism isn't enough; we need to do something about it. Therefore, Chapters 1–6 build the case against childism, while Chapters 7–10 introduce an action plan of ways to challenge it.

The first chapter in this book is one of two halves, starting with an introduction to who I am and why I have been drawn to this work, and, indeed, why you should trust me as your tour guide, and closing with an exploration of the laws in place that should, theoretically, protect children against discrimination, and how well they do their job. Chapter 2 turns back the clock, with a look at the history of childism and those who popularised the childist childcare techniques that are still commonly used by parents and carers today. In Chapters 3 and 4, we will look at sleep and discipline – two areas of child-raising that are arguably the most childist – and how their management is in direct conflict with child rights and needs. When children's needs for attachment, connection and validation are consistently unfulfilled as they grow, cycles of childism are perpetuated into the next generation. This is why it is so important to consider the impact of childism at such an early stage of childhood, regardless of how long ago we may have left that stage behind in our own lives.

We continue to build the case against childism in Chapter 5, this time turning our attention to our governments and politicians to consider what I term 'state-sponsored childism'; no book about childism would be complete without a section on childcare, education, mental-health support and the impact of putting profits before people. Moving on to Chapter 6, we will ask questions about children's right to privacy and how those raised in an online world, where their every move can be recorded and broadcast to thousands of strangers without their consent (or even knowledge) are facing new erosions of their rights, and on a scale never seen before.

The remainder of the book sets out what we can all do, armed with a new awareness of childism, to call for and bring about positive change. Chapter 7 asks you to imagine a world without childism, considering what our childcare, education, mental-health support and more would look like if they were truly designed to meet the needs of children and their families. Chapter 8 discusses how to tackle those who loudly declare 'It never did me any harm!' and dismiss the idea and very existence of childism. In this chapter, we will also consider how to work with people who declare that those who believe in childism are woke snowflakes, and understand what causes somebody to hold this viewpoint. Chapter 9 introduces my blueprint for an anti-childist society and invites you to become a cycle breaker, with advice on how best to do this while also considering your own needs. Finally, Chapter 10 is focused on myth busting – providing rebuttals to the comments and criticisms you will so often hear from anti-childism detractors.

My hope is that by the end of this book you will not only understand childism and be fired up to tackle it, but you will also know how to do so. Being anti-childist is about considering how we treat children today, being aware of and removing discrimination, in order to give children a voice and help them to know that they matter, just as much as adults. Childhood isn't just practice for adulthood – children are important now. And the more we understand and accept this, the more likely it will be that they will grow up feeling happy and confident, knowing that their voices matter.

If we want to leave a better world for our children, we need to consider the way we treat them, and to do this we need to understand, and ultimately accept, that we ourselves weren't treated very well by adults during our own childhoods. Once we become aware of the childism that *we* faced and that it is omnipresent in the world today, we can either remain part of the problem, doing nothing to solve it, or we can use any resulting discomfort as fuel to fire us into making a change and breaking the childist cycle for our own children and those who follow.

Which will you choose?

At this point I feel I should, perhaps, apologise to you because this book is going to make you feel uncomfortable and angry, but it's necessary. It is a call to arms: we must change things.

Are you ready to be part of an anti-childist revolution? Then it's time to go down the rabbit hole ...

Chapter 1

The Case Against Childism

A person's a person no matter how small.
DR SEUSS, from *Horton Hears a Who!*

When I had my first child, in 2002, I struggled to follow the mainstream parenting advice of the time, particularly when it came to sleep. My son was easily the worst sleeper of all the babies I came across in the baby groups we attended. The other parents were able to put their babies down awake in their cots in their blacked-out nurseries, give them a quick kiss on the cheek, then walk out and close the door. Their babies were capable of the miraculous skill of 'self-soothing', while mine would cling to me desperately. He wailed when I put him down, his arms reaching up for me, big brown, teary eyes pleading with me to pick him up again. My baby's sleep and feeding schedules were erratic and unpredictable, while theirs would sleep and feed to the clock, with military predictability.

Desperate to 'fix' my baby, I turned to books and online advice that urged me to leave him to cry for a few minutes, while I waited, physically unresponsive, nearby. Apparently, in my quest to soothe my son, I had created bad habits that we now had to break. We lasted for one horrible, heartbreaking night. I couldn't bear to put him through any more trauma. Reluctantly, I continued to meet his needs for physical contact throughout the day and night, all the while feeling that I was somehow a worse parent than those with the perfect sleeping babies because I had failed to do what was best for him.

My son quickly grew into a toddler and my worries moved on from sleep to be replaced by concerns about his tantrums. Here, the books, television experts and online chat groups told me to reward him when he was well behaved with stickers on a chart displayed on our fridge door, and to punish him by sending him for time out when he was 'naughty'. I struggled to make him stay in one place when we attempted time out, so one day, in desperation, I learned that if I shut him in our small entrance porch, he could not open the door handle and escape. For a week, I faithfully took him to the porch and closed the door every time he misbehaved. I would stand the other side of the door, while he howled and pleaded with me to let him out, timing two minutes – a minute for each year of his age, as advised. This seemed even worse than the sleep training we'd attempted. It physically hurt my heart to hear him begging me to open the door, and when his time was up, he once again clung to me, heaving big sobs for what felt like hours.

Once again, I abandoned the technique advocated by so many and decided that I just wasn't strong enough to follow the advice. I had failed to sleep train my son and now I was failing to discipline him. I felt like a social pariah at baby and toddler groups, with the placid, good-sleeper babies and compliant toddlers. Eventually, I stopped going to them. Instead, I stayed at home, where I didn't feel pressure to follow the popular childcare methods that produced such 'easy', 'well-behaved' children.

As the months and years went by, I learned that the best way to help my son (and his three siblings who followed) to sleep and to regulate his emotions, was through connection, meeting his needs and helping him to feel safe and secure. I began to learn his triggers and how to avoid them, and how to de-escalate him when his big feelings threatened to boil over. We were both so much happier. Slowly, I learned to trust my instincts to nurture my son and to place his needs above the opinions of others. And the more I did so, the more I resented the advice I had received – not just from books, strangers on the Internet and the television parenting experts of the time, but from healthcare professionals, too.

Talk of 'ignore, punish, praise and reward' and teaching self-soothing was everywhere. Finally, I began to question the commonly held wisdom more than I questioned my own instincts and my son's behaviour. I realised that the advice *felt* wrong because it *was* wrong. It was all about ignoring a child's needs, not meeting them. It was all about disconnecting, rather than connecting. It was about compliance over compassion and forcing independence before meeting the primal need for dependence. The advice didn't work for me. But perhaps most importantly, it didn't work for my son.

I grew angry at the messages so prevalent in society which led me to try to raise my son in a way that felt instinctively wrong to both me and him. However, these experiences also planted a seed – one that would take a further five years to begin to sprout and another two decades to come to fruition. They became the fuel behind my desire to raise awareness of the way society discriminates against children and their needs in an attempt to prioritise the wants and wishes of adults. While I would dearly love to relive those early years free of self-doubt, to enjoy every precious snuggle with my son and to treat him with the full respect he truly deserved from the moment he was born, I wouldn't be doing what I do today without them. The realisation of the terrible childism that exists in our society today, from the very moment a baby is born, is the inspiration for everything I have done in my professional life since.

In 2007, I started to run classes in my home, supporting parents to use what I called 'gentle parenting' methods. We spoke about the importance of nurturance, empathy and meeting the needs of our children. We spoke of respecting babies and children as we would respect adults. Through word of mouth, these small classes quickly grew and I developed gentle-parenting workshops that I delivered, and still do to this day, to thousands of parents. I spoke of tackling sleep and tricky behaviour with a mindset of placing the child at the heart of the conversation, removing the discrimination towards children that features so heavily in most parenting advice. In 2011, I began to write my first parenting book, with the aim of producing the book that I wished I had read myself as a new parent – one that honoured my baby's needs and my instincts. That first book focused on gentle parenting from the very beginning of life, because that is where childism begins, and this is the reason why you will find two whole chapters devoted to the discriminatory treatment of children under three here. One book quickly led to another, and another, and now, fourteen books on, I have become known as 'the inventor of gentle parenting'. While the label is flattering, it isn't true. I simply put into words what parents did for centuries naturally before the so-called experts came along and told them that they were doing everything wrong.

As I reflect on my personal and professional past, I realise that everything I have done and experienced to date has led me to writing this book. My passion for battling injustice and empowering parents to trust their instincts and treat children with the same respect we would show an adult is, ultimately, a calling to make as many people as possible aware of childism and how we can change it. This anti-childism message is the 'why' behind the 'how to' of the gentle-parenting messages I am so well known for, and which we will discuss later in this book. As Dr Seuss so succinctly said in the quote at the beginning of this chapter, 'A person's a person no matter how small' – the rights of children should matter just as much as those of adults.

Origins of the word 'childism'?

The word 'childism' was first used by doctors Chester Pierce and Gail Allen in 1975, in a psychiatric journal article.[1] They defined it as 'the automatic presumption of superiority of any adult over any child; it results in the adult's needs, desires, hopes and fears taking unquestioned precedence over those of the child'. The idea, sadly, received little attention over the following three decades, until 2012, when the late American academic and psychotherapist Elisabeth Young-Bruehl published her book *Childism: Confronting Prejudice Against Children*.[2] Young-Bruehl introduced the concept of childism, saying:

> ... we are accustomed to thinking in terms of prejudice against women, against people of color, against other groups that are 'targets of prejudice' as we call them, in Western society, and we accept the idea that struggles against sexism and racism have been going on since the eighteenth century and will have to keep going on if these prejudices are ever to be overcome. But prejudice against children? Who even acknowledges its existence?

Young-Bruehl ultimately called for society to reconsider the way it views childhood and treats children, with an emphasis on ending child incarceration, reducing child abuse and reducing the voting age to sixteen. While Young-Bruehl's work was an academic success, it sadly did not reach a wider audience in the general public. My hope with this book, taking inspiration from the work of Pierce, Allen and Young-Bruehl, is to help bring the word 'childism' to the forefront of the vocabularies of as many adults as possible. I believe it is too important a concept to remain in the exclusive domain of academia. It's time that it was discussed as much as other 'isms' and forms of discrimination in society today. Everybody needs to be aware of the word and what it means.

Why childism is harmful

Perhaps the most damaging aspect of childism is that it impacts every single one of us and therefore every single adult who has ever had, or ever will have, children will have been affected by it, whether they are aware of it or not. It is insidious. Those who make our laws and write rules and guidelines that affect children will have experienced it. Those who decide public budgets and expenditure have been affected by it. And those who are meant to protect the rights of children have lived through it. But why does this matter? Because it means we are all a little bit damaged, whether we realise it or not, and our childhood wiring tends to shape our subconscious beliefs – that children are somehow worth less and deserve less than adults – in such a way that we continue the cycle of discrimination, simply because we don't know any different. We relive what we experienced in childhood when we have children of our own and our buried beliefs influence every action we take as parents.

Most adults struggle to regulate their emotions well. We frequently shout, sulk, threaten, argue, worry, ignore, suppress, detract and distract when we are faced with big feelings and difficult situations. We struggle with our mental health and our relationships, we struggle to strike a good work–life balance, we struggle to set and uphold boundaries to protect our physical and psychological health, we struggle to ask for help and we struggle with our own self-talk and self-esteem. These struggles are almost all due to the fact that the adults in our lives didn't help us to regulate our emotions when we were children. They stem from the times when we were left alone to cry, when we were scolded for being too loud, too much, too needy. When we were led to believe that *we* were the problem. The roots are in the times when we didn't get the human touch we needed, when we felt misunderstood, unheard and unloved and grew to believe that a part of us was therefore unlovable and not worthy of respect. I'm not saying any of this to blame our parents and carers – because they are just as much victims of childism as us, dysregulated from their own childist upbringings. We will talk about this much more in Chapter 8, with a focus on understanding the adults in our lives, rather than blaming and shaming them (because the latter helps nobody to move forwards), but for now it's just important to recognise that we have all been impacted by childism, whether we realise it or not.

What happens when individuals grow up with their need for love, nurturance, support and dependence as children having been unmet, believing that children are somehow less than adults? How can they, as adults, fully meet their children's needs for the same things? The answer is they can't – not without some work – which is why so many parents struggle with anger, frustration and short tempers around their children. To raise well-regulated children, we must first acknowledge that our emotional needs in childhood weren't fully met and, as a result, we struggle to regulate ourselves, especially around our children. We must acknowledge the existence of childism. This is difficult and often painful, and so the awareness, or 'wokeness', as some mistakenly refer to it, remains buried and the cycle of discrimination continues. Society continues to advocate for the needs of adults over those of children, sleep training being a great example of this (something we will discuss in depth in Chapter 3). The common ways in which we discipline children today are also an example of prioritising the rights of adults over those of children, with resulting harmful outcomes (we will discuss the research into the harm caused here in Chapter 4).

In reality, the most equitable answer to any parenting dilemma is surely one that considers the needs of both parent and child and tries to find an acceptable middle ground. Once again, however, for this to happen, adults must genuinely consider the rights of children and break free from the delusion that we treat them well in our society. As the saying goes, 'hurt people hurt people', and a whole generation of adults who, as children, grew to believe that they didn't matter as much as the adults in their lives, are likely to perpetuate this belief, and the hurt, with any children in their care.

Gentle parenting – the key to combatting childism?

You've probably come across gentle parenting before, or the term, anyway. Sadly, though, a lot of articles and videos that claim to be discussing and illustrating gentle parenting are uninformed. It is commonly reduced to a series of statements, or actions, which cover what to do or say to children in a certain situation. This isn't gentle parenting. Similarly, many seem to believe that it is a style of parenting devoid of discipline, allowing children to do anything they want, prioritising their needs and rights above their parents', until parents become perpetually exhausted martyrs. This isn't gentle parenting either.

What does real gentle parenting look like? In short, it is a philosophy, an ethos, where the rights and needs of both adults and children are considered, and where a healthy balance is drawn. It hinges on three words: understanding, empathy and respect. Understanding normal child development and behaviour and deviations from it in order to have realistic expectations of a child; empathising with children and attempting to see the world through their eyes, so that we can connect with them to collaboratively solve any problems together; and respecting children as the individual, worthy beings that they are, rather than seeing them as second-class citizens or 'adults in the making'. Gentle parenting isn't about a set of superficial discipline tactics or rehearsed stock phrases to say to children, as so many articles and videos would have it. It's a mindset, or rather a mind shift. If I'm asked to describe it in one short sentence, I simply say, 'It's treating children the way in which you wish you had been treated yourself as a child.'

In my opinion, gentle parenting is the answer to combatting childism – because if we fully respect children, we not only respect their needs, but we also respect their human rights.

Child rights are human rights

Before we go any further, I feel it would be a good idea to take a quick whistle-stop tour of human rights, specifically those involving the rights of children. I believe it is impossible to talk about childism without first understanding the legal rights children should have and considering whether these are met or breached in society today.

Human rights, or the belief that we are all legally entitled to the same basic rights from birth through to death, are universal moral principles that are enshrined by law. They strive for fairness, justice and equality and aim to protect individuals of all ages from discrimination. They cover areas such as the right to receive an education, the right to privacy and the right to freedom of expression. Importantly, we are protected from discrimination in respect of upholding and following these rights, too.

The human rights that so many of us take for granted today exist thanks to work that took place after the end of the Second World War in an attempt to prevent a recurrence of the horrors from that time. In 1948, the United Nations General Assembly met to adopt the Universal Declaration of Human Rights (abbreviated to UDHR).[3] This lengthy document sought to enshrine the universal rights of all individuals into law. Stating that we are all 'born free and equal in dignity and rights ... regardless of nationality, place of residence, gender, national or ethnic origin, colour, religion, language, or any other status'. While the UDHR protects rights for all humans, they are not specific to age, and therefore do not separate child and adult rights. Considering their unique needs, children need further protection legally, with rights that are specific to them.

The history of child rights

The Geneva Declaration of the Rights of the Child is often termed the original declaration of child rights,[4] written by Eglantyne Jebb, a British teacher and social reformer who was passionate about the treatment of starving children in Germany and Austria during the First World War, when the troops of the Allied forces prevented the passage of much-needed food and medical supplies. Jebb felt strongly that children should not suffer because of the war and campaigned to parliament for change. In 1919, the charity Save the Children was born. After the war had ended, in 1924, Jebb joined world leaders at the Genevan League of Nations Convention to share her idea of a declaration of child rights. The declaration was quickly adopted legally. Sadly, Jebb died only nine years later, at the age of fifty-two – however, her legacy lives on in the shape of Save the Children, which is still operational and influential today.

Building upon and inspired by Jebb's Geneva declaration, with child-specific rights in mind, the United Nations Convention on the Rights of the Child (or UNCRC) treaty was adopted by the UN General Assembly in 1989.[5] It is a legally binding agreement for members (countries) to uphold the specific rights of children and, importantly, the UNCRC is of utmost significance when we consider childism and any attempts to stop it. The UNCRC is regarded as having been enormously effective in improving the lives of children around the world and has influenced political policies on a global level. It is not perfect, however, and many countries do not uphold its tenets, whether purposefully or unknowingly. In addition, the world in which we live is rapidly changing, with new threats and potential discrimination towards children arising, for instance those posed by access to the Internet.

The UNCRC has been formally signed and adopted (known as ratification) by all United Nations countries, bar one – the United States of America. The USA has signed the UNCRC, which indicates its intention to ratify it at some point in the future; however, ratification has not moved forwards outside of individual states. This is, in part, because of opposition from religious organisations in the USA who disagree with the contents of the UNCRC and argue that it would meddle too much with individual family choices and decisions, and potentially erode parental rights.

What does the UNCRC contain?

The UNCRC includes fifty-four sections (known as articles), each covering different aspects of child rights. Overall, these articles protect children from physical and emotional harm, ensure they receive an education and have the right to be heard and express their opinions, in order that each can live to their full potential, without discrimination due to age, race, sex, religion, abilities or other characteristics and safeguard their rights to a relationship with their parents, without undue separation from them.

Although all the articles are important, some are critical when it comes to childism and the contents of this book, including the following:

- **Article 12** Covering the rights of children to hold and express their own views, it states: 'Parties shall assure to the child who is capable of forming his or her own views the right to express those views freely in all matters affecting the child, the views of the child being given due weight in accordance with the age and maturity of the child.'

- **Article 13** Covering the rights of children to freedom of expression, it states: 'This right shall include freedom to seek, receive and impart information and ideas of all kinds, regardless of frontiers, either orally, in writing or in print, in the form of art, or through any other media of the child's choice.'

- **Article 19** Covering the rights of children to protection from physical and emotional violence, it states: 'Parties shall take all appropriate legislative, administrative, social and educational measures to protect the child from all forms of physical or mental violence, injury or abuse, neglect or negligent treatment, maltreatment or exploitation, including sexual abuse, while in the care of parent(s), legal guardian(s) or any other person who has the care of the child.'

- **Article 23** Covering the rights of children with disabilities, which include learning disabilities and neurodivergence, it states: 'Parties recognize that a mentally or physically disabled child should enjoy a full and decent life, in conditions which ensure dignity, promote self-reliance and facilitate the child's active participation in the community.'

- **Article 27** Covering the rights of children to a good standard of living, it states: 'Parties recognize the right of every child to a standard of living adequate for the child's physical, mental, spiritual, moral and social development.'

- **Article 28** Covering the rights of children to a good education, with one section stating: 'Parties shall take all appropriate measures to ensure that school discipline is administered in a manner consistent with the child's human dignity and in conformity with the present Convention.'

- **Article 29** Continuing the rights of education, the first section states: 'Parties agree that the education of the child shall be directed to the development of the child's personality, talents and mental and physical abilities to their fullest potential.'
- **Article 31** Covering the rights of children to free time, it states: 'Parties recognize the right of the child to rest and leisure, to engage in play and recreational activities appropriate to the age of the child and to participate freely in cultural life and the arts.'

I won't go into further detail about the UNCRC here, but we'll be picking up discussion of these articles again a little later in the chapter and again in Chapter 5, when we discuss state-sponsored childism, specifically relating to education, mental health and special-educational-needs provision, and economic help provided to families today.

Child rights in the United Kingdom

With the UK's ratification of the UNCRC in 1991, you would imagine that child rights are the same as all other human rights in the UK. Indeed, the UNCRC should protect all children from any actions which infringe their human rights and prevent them from being on the receiving end of poor treatment due to their age. Unfortunately, this is not the case in many countries, including the UK, especially when it comes to three key areas where child rights are not equal to those of adults and where children are actively discriminated against due to their age. These are:

- corporal punishment
- the age of consent and body autonomy
- voting age.

Corporal punishment in the United Kingdom

Since the late 1990s, government power in the UK has been decentralised through a process known as devolution. This means that the ability to make decisions and certain laws for each of the countries in the UK has moved from being centralised in parliament in Westminster, London to separate governments and parliaments in England, Wales, Scotland and Northern Ireland. In turn, this means that the countries that comprise the UK have different laws when it comes to using physical punishment as a form of disciplining children. The laws at the time of writing are as follows:

Scotland

Smacking children was made illegal in Scotland in November 2020, with all forms of physical discipline – including smacking, spanking, slapping and tapping – being prohibited by law, meaning that any of these acts would be treated in the same way as they would if they were done to an adult, i.e. as physical assault.[6] Those witnessing physical assault of children are encouraged to report the crime to the Scottish Police.

Wales

The Welsh government made physical discipline of children – including smacking, slapping, hitting and shaking – illegal in March 2022.[7] The law applies to everybody, regardless of whether they are the child's parent or unrelated, and also to visitors to

Wales, even if they are from other countries. As with Scottish law, anybody witnessing physical discipline towards children is encouraged to report the crime to social services or the police.

England and Northern Ireland

In England and Northern Ireland, it is illegal for a professional, such as nursery or teaching staff, to use physical discipline on children. However, parents and legal guardians are permitted to hit, slap, smack, spank, shove and shake their children, so long as it is deemed 'reasonable punishment'.[8] Reasonable punishment is open to interpretation, however, and many believe physical punishment to be reasonable if no lasting bruises or cuts are left on the skin and the child's actions were deemed bad enough to warrant it.

In Scotland, a group of parents are campaigning to overturn the Scottish smacking ban in order to be legally allowed to smack their children if they personally consider the punishment 'reasonable' (the group is called 'Be Reasonable'); they believe that smacking and hitting are not the same thing, and that smacking is justified if children are between two and six years of age and do not understand or cannot rationalise verbal forms of discipline.[9] You have to wonder why parents believe that a young child will learn from being struck if they lack rational thinking skills and cannot learn from being spoken to. This argument seems to be the very antithesis of being reasonable.

Speaking at the time of the Welsh ban, in 2022, then education secretary Nadhim Zahawi stated that he did not want to make physical punishment illegal in England, because he did not want to 'end up in a world where the state is nannying people about how they bring up their children'.[10] In a YouGov poll held in 2021, 34 per cent of respondents believed that physical punishment is still an effective way to improve a child's behaviour, with 41 per cent of respondents who had at least one child under the age of eighteen believing that parents should legally be allowed to hit their children.[11] We'll talk a lot more about smacking, and other forms of discipline, in Chapter 4, but for now I would like to put to you two questions:

1. Is smacking/slapping/hitting/spanking/tapping children in contravention of article 19 of the United Nations Convention on the Rights of the Child (see pages 18–21 for a reminder)?
2. Are child rights really human rights if it is illegal for us to hit anybody over the age of eighteen, for any reason, and yet in England and Northern Ireland we may hit children so long as the punishment is deemed 'reasonable'?

The age of consent and body autonomy

In the UK, a child under the age of eighteen is not allowed to get a tattoo, even if they have parental consent. In the USA, there is no overarching federal law concerning the age of consent for receiving a tattoo; however, individual state laws (in all states) stipulate that the minimum age is eighteen. In Scotland, it is illegal for a child up to the age of sixteen to get their ears or other parts of their body pierced without parental consent, yet in England and Wales, there is no minimum age of consent for piercing children. One in six children is believed to have had their ears pierced in the UK by the time they are six years old. The question is: who is giving consent for this to happen? The children? Or their parents?

Gillick competence is a term often used to decide whether a child has the mental capacity and understanding to give informed consent for medical procedures. It is often used alongside something known as Fraser guidelines. Both Gillick competence and Fraser guidelines originate from a legal case in the 1980s, which sought to determine whether a sixteen-year-old girl could be given oral contraceptive pills without her mother's consent (the case was known as Gillick v. West Norfolk and Wisbech Area Health Authority).[12] The outcome of the case was that doctors were allowed to prescribe contraceptives to the girl, and therefore other children under sixteen years old, without parental consent, if the child was deemed able to give informed consent. Fraser guidelines are used to determine whether children have the necessary maturity to make medical decisions relating to their sexual health, whereas Gillick competence is used for decisions relating to medical and other issues as well. There is no lower age limit for either Gillick competence or meeting the Fraser guidelines, and no set list of questions to ask. Instead, they are assessed on a case-by-case basis looking at the understanding, maturity, rationality and emotional skills of the child. Many would argue that it is uncommon for a child to be assessed as Gillick competent before their teen years, although theoretically there is nothing to stop a much younger child being assessed as competent if they are genuinely thought to possess the ability to make a rational, informed decision.

I'd now like to ask three questions, considering the concept of Gillick competence and child body autonomy.

1. If a child is too young to be determined as Gillick competent, should their parent or guardian be able to make choices for them that may carry pain and risk, if those choices are merely cosmetic and solely for the enjoyment of adults – say, deciding to pierce a baby's ears?

2. If a sixteen-year-old, who is mature and would be considered Gillick competent (meaning they fully understand all risks and the long-term consequences), would like a tattoo, is it childist if UK law makes it illegal for them to get one until they turn eighteen?

3. If a parent or guardian can give consent for their child's body to be cosmetically modified from infancy (as is the case with ear piercing), is it childist that that same child cannot legally choose to cosmetically modify their own body (say, with a tattoo) until they turn eighteen?

Voting age

Voting for who you would like to run your constituency and – perhaps most importantly – your country is largely restricted around the world to adults only, meaning children, who are likely to be affected for the longest time by political decisions, are prohibited from voting in most countries. There are a few exceptions, these being Austria, Brazil, Cuba, Ecuador, Ethiopia, Guernsey, the Isle of Man, Malta, Nicaragua, Scotland (in local elections, the Scottish referendum and those relating to Scottish parliament only) and Wales (in local elections and those relating to Welsh parliament only). Brazil reduced the age of voting eligibility to sixteen in 1988 (coming into force in 1989); Austria became the first country in Europe to change their voting laws when they reduced the voting age to sixteen in 2011; and Scotland's devolved powers saw the voting age drop to sixteen in 2014. A handful of countries, including Greece and Indonesia, allow seventeen-year-olds to vote. At the turn of this century, many states in the USA debated lowering the voting age (including California and Florida), however no change was ultimately made.

One argument commonly used to limit the vote to over-eighteens is that children do not pay taxes. However, income tax is not restricted to a certain age – rather, it is based on earnings. Sixteen-year-olds are legally allowed to work for others, or become self-employed, and will pay income tax if their earnings are high enough. Similarly, many sixteen-year-olds undertake government-backed paid apprenticeships, contributing to the national economy. If a child is earning and understands politics (arguably, those sixteen- and seventeen-year-olds studying for politics A-level have a better understanding than many adults), it makes no sense to prevent them from having any involvement in what happens in their future, especially when we consider that sixteen-year-olds are almost always considered to be Gillick competent, too. The UK's EU (Brexit) referendum is a prime example of not giving children a voice about important matters that will directly affect their future. Of those eighteen- to twenty-four-year-olds who voted, 74 per cent voted to remain. Contrast this to the 42 per cent of sixty-five-year-olds and over who voted to remain. Of course, we do not know how sixteen- and seventeen-year-olds would have voted, but it is not unreasonable to assume, given the trends shown by the majority of lower ages voting to remain, that over 75 per cent of them would have voted that way, too.

I would like to put to you three questions here:

1. Article 12 of the UN Convention on the Rights of the Child states: 'Parties shall assure to the child who is capable of forming his or her own views the right to express those views freely in all matters affecting the child, the views of the child being given due weight in accordance with the age and maturity of the child.' Is restricting the voting age to over-eighteens potentially a contravention of article 12?
2. Should a well-informed sixteen-year-old be allowed to vote for their future? Especially if that sixteen-year-old works and pays income tax, and would also be considered Gillick competent?
3. Are countries who restrict votes to adults only genuinely respecting child rights, or are they childist?

We will come back to the childism shown in politics and government actions again in Chapter 5, when we discuss what

I call 'state-sponsored childism' – there is a lot more to be said about it.

Child rights are human rights, take two

I'd like to end this chapter with the idea that child rights are human rights. Children are humans, just like you and me, and while they may need special rights to protect them, these should not be at the expense of their basic human rights. It makes no sense that you cannot hit your partner, friend, colleague, parent or a random person in the street in England or Northern Ireland without breaking the law and potentially being convicted of common assault, or worse, yet you are legally allowed to strike a child if the punishment is considered 'reasonable'.

Children, who arguably have more passion and political knowledge than the average adult are not allowed to have a say in their future by voting, even though the UN Convention on the Rights of the Child is clear that their voices should be heard. And despite having specific rights protecting children's bodies, parents are still allowed to make holes in them to insert jewellery to make them look more cosmetically pleasing to adults. Child rights are not human rights – not yet, anyway.

We have all been children; we should be their biggest champions. But as we discussed at the beginning of this chapter, many of us weren't treated very well as children, often causing us to unconsciously perpetuate the same treatment and beliefs: that children are somehow worth less and are therefore entitled to less than adults. We seem to view adulthood as life, and childhood as a mere rehearsal for it, with only the fully fledged adult performers receiving respect for their rights.

In essence, aiming to stop discrimination towards children

means honouring our own needs, making peace with our past, trying to do the right thing by children in the present and fighting for a better future for the next generation. In a world full of childist beliefs, it takes bravery to stand up and speak out. There are a lot of damaged people in our society, and until now they have been allowed to have the loudest voices, ridiculing those who disagree. But now is the time for change – and to change the future, we must understand where we have come from. We must study the childist roots of our society in order to weed them out and allow a better future to grow and blossom. Chapter 2 takes us back to the past – are you ready to go back for the future of children? Then read on . . .

Chapter 2

The History of Childism

It's been a long time since universal
suffrage, and I'm sick of the old white men
running the show.

CATE BLANCHETT, actor[1]

Have you ever desperately tried to follow a piece of parenting or childcare advice that just didn't feel right? Much like I did, as shared with you in the last chapter. Maybe a health or education professional advised you to follow a certain discipline tip that left you feeling as if you'd been too harsh on your child? Or maybe a family member encouraged you to leave your baby crying in their cot for a few minutes, in the hope of improving their sleep? Perhaps a stranger on the Internet pushed their views on getting children to eat vegetables, leaving you doubting yourself and wondering if, actually, your inability to be firmer was the cause of your child's fussy eating? Or maybe your teenager's school suggested that you need to crack down on them with stricter consequences in order to better control their behaviour?

As parents and carers, our instincts are strong. We innately feel drawn to nurture children, to protect them. And yet so much advice today centres on hurting them, whether physically or emotionally, to get them to behave as we expect and want them to. When we are advised to treat children in a way that goes against our instincts, instead of trusting our gut feelings and following them, most of the time we push on with trying to implement the childcare technique in question because we believe that we are doing it 'for the best'.

Whenever I work with a new mother who is struggling with matrescence (the psychological transition to motherhood), there is always an element of her grappling with the innate drive to 'mother' her newborn through love, responsivity and unlimited physical touch. These internal drives are frequently undermined by external advice to not spoil the baby, to avoid creating bad habits, to encourage independence by not picking the baby up too much and to get the baby into a timed routine for both eating and sleeping. Mothers understandably struggle with this, because it is at odds with what their hearts and genetic programming tell them to do. The saddest thing here is that so many vulnerable new mothers believe this advice, and by extension, they also believe that there must be something wrong with them for not being able to be firm enough to do what they now consider is 'best' for their babies. It's rare that I meet a new father struggling with the same thoughts and feelings. In part, I think this is because men are less likely to go looking for this external advice and validation; they don't tend to join parenting discussion groups or follow parenting accounts on social media (of the over 50,000 members in my online parenting discussion groups, fewer than 3 per cent identify as male) and they don't tend to buy parenting books or search websites for parenting advice. It's also far less likely for them to be on the receiving end of unsolicited childcare advice.

Why childism is a feminist issue

The fact that men rarely receive unsolicited parenting advice highlights the unconscious bias held by so many that caring, particularly unpaid care such as raising children, is a woman's job.

Men are still all too commonly seen as the family breadwinners, with little perceived psychological involvement in the role of raising their children. Instead, women carry the bulk of the parenting mental load alone. When fathers are involved in everyday care for their children, they often receive praise ('It's wonderful he's so involved with the children when he's so busy with work!'); when mothers do exactly the same, however, they are often criticised ('She's trying to have it all with both work and children – it's not fair to the children'). Similarly, mothers who work are commonly referred to as 'working mums', yet nobody refers to fathers who work as 'working dads'. Fathers with their own businesses are entrepreneurs, while mothers are mumpreneurs. Women are defined by their parenting status, while men are not.

There is a clear link between the discrimination of women, particularly mothers, and that of children. If children are seen as somehow less than adults, then devoting time to raising them is not seen as a worthwhile job. Historically, it has almost exclusively been men giving childcare advice to women. Childcare expertise sat firmly under the patriarchal thumb of privileged, highly educated male experts. The most influential childcare books of the past century have almost all been written by men, and while women took on the apparently menial work of the day-to-day care of children, men took the position of expert, telling them what to do. Maternal instincts have been no match for the power held by the males in our society, who believed that both children and their mothers needed to be controlled. If children are not truly valued and respected by society, then it follows that their primary caregivers – mothers (or women) are not either, or vice versa.

While there is a slow shift towards valuing the matriarchs of the family once again, much of the childcare advice parents receive today is a hangover from popular male childcare experts of the past. If we treated children as equals, we would have to admit how important childcare, or indeed all forms of care, is. We would have to value women as primary child carers and we would have to view childcare as one of the most important jobs in society today, which would have far-reaching financial consequences for the childcare industry and its funding. Alas, these beliefs directly challenge patriarchy, which requires men to be seen as the most important in society and politics, and childcare as a 'lesser' occupation in order to justify continually underfunding childcare. Naturally, this bias impacts the confidence and self-esteem of mothers who are struggling to juggle everybody's needs in a society that doesn't fully support them or their children.

Childism is a feminist issue, and yet it is one rarely raised by the most outspoken feminists of today.

How historical male childcare advice perpetuates childism

The ideas that underpin much childcare advice today, whether about sleep training for babies and tantrums in toddlers or the discipline used commonly in schools and handling unruly teens, are echoes of the childist advice given by male childcare experts over the last two centuries. We may believe that we are following recommendations that are current and informed by recent research and scientific understanding, especially when it comes from professionals or is instigated by institutions such as schools; however, this is often not the case.

Let's take a look at some common beliefs that run through childcare advice today and consider their underlying childist principles. Once again, the advice focuses on caring for the youngest of children, because babyhood is the place where childism begins and, arguably, is at its most shocking. The practices followed in infancy, however, continue throughout the whole of childhood and affect all children, whatever their age. As you read through the next few pages, perhaps you could consider how the messages of the historic male childcare experts, written for babies and toddlers, continue to have an impact on common beliefs about the care and treatment of older children.

Common belief: Don't spoil a baby by picking them up too much; they need to learn to be independent!

We are a society obsessed with fostering independence in children from as early as possible. Parents are commonly advised that it is best for their baby if they learn to spend time alone and are able to settle to sleep with no adult intervention. Similarly, detachment is encouraged in the very early years in order that children learn to be happy without their parents: for instance when they start nursery. These ideas, however, are in direct contrast with what we know is best for children – that is, to form a strong attachment with their primary caregivers which, in turn, provides them with a 'secure base' from which to explore the world around them with confidence. True independence cannot be forced; it happens naturally when the child's needs for dependence have been fulfilled. Advice to encourage early separation is incredibly misguided, but very common. Where does it stem from? Perhaps the main source here is the American psychologist John B. Watson, who did most of his work in the 1920s.

Commonly known as the founding father of behaviourism, his most famous work being about the process of conditioning, Watson believed that all behaviour during infancy and childhood (and thus into adulthood) was conditioned by the experiences that occurred in the child's life, both good and, especially, bad. Watson's most famous experiment studying this process of conditioning is known as 'Little Albert'. 'Albert' (likely a pseudonym) was only eleven months old when Watson began to experiment on him, and while there is no certainty around Albert's identity, it is likely he was the son of a nurse who worked with Watson. Watson's hypothesis was that an infant was born a blank slate and that they could be taught to fear various things through a process of conditioning to unrelated objects. To achieve this process of conditioning fear, Watson would sit behind Albert and bang an iron bar loudly close to his head whenever the child was presented with something innocuous, such as a fluffy rabbit.

Using Albert as proof, Watson held that parents conditioned fear, clinginess and anxiety in their children by over-nurturing them and holding them too much. Regarding nurturing children, Watson wrote the following in his book *The Psychological Care of Infant and Child*, published in 1928[2]:

Let your behaviour always be objective and kindly firm. Never hug and kiss them, never let them sit in your lap. If you must, kiss them once on the forehead when they say goodnight. Shake hands with them in the morning. Give them a pat on the head if they have made an extraordinarily good job of a difficult task.

Watson considered that if babies weren't picked up, kissed, cuddled and spoiled with too much affection, they would grow to be confident, independent and happy, free of the separation anxiety that we now know is a normal stage of infant development, indicating a baby has a secure attachment with his or her primary caregivers. Watson was so concerned that mothers shouldn't ruin their babies that he titled a whole chapter of his book 'The dangers of too much mother love'.

Watson held that many emotional problems faced by grown adults occurred because of over-coddling in infancy and childhood. This intense nurturing was believed to create adults who were unable to stick at anything, with low resilience to hard work. Watson's solution to prevent the modern problem of over-coddled adults was to teach toughness and independence from the moment a baby could crawl, by fencing off an area of grass in the garden in which to leave the baby for as long as possible. Parents were advised:

> ... give it a sand pile, and be sure to dig some small holes in the yard, so it has to crawl in and out of them. Let it learn to overcome difficulties almost from the moment of birth. The child should learn to conquer difficulties away from your watchful eye ... If your heart is too tender and you must watch the child, make yourself a peep-hole so that you can see it without being seen.

Almost one hundred years after Watson's words were written, we are still hung up on the idea of making children resilient and avoiding creating 'snowflakes'.

Common belief: Never feed or rock a baby to sleep, or you will create bad habits

If you read any article on how to encourage a baby or toddler to 'sleep through the night', you will undoubtedly encounter a section that warns against feeding or rocking to sleep. Commonly, these practices are described as 'bad habits' which prevent the child from forming so-called healthy sleep cues. Of course, this is entirely wrong – feeding and rocking to sleep are perhaps two of the best ways to soothe and settle a fractious baby or toddler, and often result in the speediest of sleep onsets. How can something so physiologically normal be considered a bad habit? Here, we need to look back at the work of a man known as Luther Emmett Holt.

Holt was an American physician, who had a reputation as one of the best paediatricians of his time. His book *The Care and Feeding of Children: A Catechism for the Use of Mothers and Children's Nurses*, published in 1894, was a runaway bestseller and remained the go-to manual for mothers for the next twenty-five years.[3] Much of Holt's book contains sensible advice, covering basic safety precautions to prevent accidents and illnesses. Where Holt's advice is less sound, however, is in the sections of his book covering sleep management. Holt believed that mothers interrupted their babies' sleep when they rocked or fed them to sleep. His advice was to feed the baby, darken their nursery and then put them down in their crib and leave them to fall asleep alone. He felt that rocking a baby at night was a bad habit, which would be hard to break, and that feeding a baby during the night caused broken sleep, as did picking them up if they woke and cried at night – advice that is still very much in line with sleep-training information today. Holt's advice regarding babies who were crying to be picked up was that 'it should not be further interfered with … It should simply be allowed to "cry it out". This often requires an hour, and, in extreme cases, two or three hours.' Holt was the original advocate of the 'cry-it-out' method of baby sleep training – a method still favoured by many today.

Common belief: Leaving babies and toddlers to cry at night will teach them to self-soothe and get them to sleep through the night

Mainstream sleep-training advice for babies and toddlers almost universally focuses on leaving the child to cry for a set amount of time, while their parent or carer resists picking them up. Sometimes parents are advised to wait outside the bedroom for short periods of time; other times they are advised to stand or sit next to the cot or crib and either slowly pat the child, place a hand on them or simply attempt to verbally reassure them, while avoiding physical contact. This advice stems from the work of Watson and Holt, as outlined above, but it has also been popularised by more recent male childcare experts.

Dr Christopher Green, an Australian paediatrician, released his book *Toddler Taming: A Parents' Guide to the First Four Years* in 1984.[4] The book is a beloved favourite, having been read and followed by millions of parents worldwide. Green's book did little to dispel the idea that toddlers are deliberately naughty and stubborn and are Machiavellian, master manipulators of their parents. When it came to sleep advice, Green appeared to prioritise the sleep needs of parents over the emotional and physical needs of their children. He is often referred to as 'the inventor of controlled crying' (although, arguably, this crown really belongs to Watson or Holt) and it is a technique he strongly advocated in his book, describing it as a cure for sleep problems.

With his controlled-crying method, Green advised parents to leave their toddlers to cry, suggesting that ten minutes was a good amount of time to start with. Parents should offer no comfort during this time of crying, he said, asserting that 'my controlled-crying method employs short, individually tailored periods of crying, calculated to give the maximum message, while at the same time making the child aware of what is going on'. If parents must pick the toddler up when they enter the room again, he said that they should make sure they put the child down again as soon as the crying changes to sniffing. And cuddling the toddler until they are calm is a big no-no in Green's book. As soon as the toddler is put down, the parents must leave the room and the clock starts again. After the initial period of ten minutes, parents should add another five minutes – so the first crying period = ten minutes; the second = fifteen minutes; the third = twenty minutes and so on.

Green stated that this method works to improve sleep, because the toddler learns that it simply isn't worth continuing to cry. In the original edition of the book, he said that while he disapproved of sedatives being used unnecessarily, their use could be justified as a safety valve if the controlled crying lasts for more than one hour in total.

Another male expert famed for his sleep advice is the American physician Dr Richard Ferber. Ferber has been highly influential in his field, and his research into paediatric sleep and related medical sleep disorders has been undoubtedly incredibly important and helped to further understanding normal child sleep and deviations from it. 'Ferberisation' is very similar to Green's method, involving a waiting period increasing from three minutes at the beginning of the night to thirty by the end of night seven.

Parents are advised to spend no more than one or two minutes in the bedroom when they do return to check on their child, before leaving again and starting a new period of crying. Ferber also included advice on the restriction of night feeds for babies, believing that babies over three months need very little, if any, milk at night.

For toddlers who are able to leave their beds at night, Ferber advised parents to fit a baby gate on their door so that they cannot escape their room and find their parents. Should the toddler manage to leave their room, parents should return them immediately and close the gate or door again, with as little interaction as possible. Ferber was keen for parents to win the sleep war with their children, saying:

> No matter how much he yells, how strong he is, or how well he can climb, you must be stronger than he is. If he ends up in control instead of you, the only lesson he will learn is that he can always get his way.[5]

Ferber's advice here centres on parents taking back control from their child at night and ensuring that children don't get their own way – which would presumably involve physical contact and emotional reassurance.

The ideas of Green, Ferber and other similar experts underpin almost all sleep advice given to exhausted parents of babies and toddlers today, prioritising the needs and rights of adults over those of children, focusing on early separation, avoiding physical contact and giving parents control.

Common belief: Maternal instincts are sometimes not for the best; sometimes you have to be cruel to be kind

As we discussed at the beginning of this chapter, childism has strong links with the feminist movement. Women, or mothers, are not truly valued for the physical and emotional investment they make in raising children. New mothers are often confused about following their instincts with their babies or the advice of experts who tell them to do things that conflict with what their hearts tell them to do. The roots of this go deep, with mothers struggling to mother instinctively in a patriarchal society. Once again, we can trace back these struggles to the advice of several historical male childcare experts.

Watson postulated whether children would be better off raised in an expert institution, away from the psychological damage novice parents could inflict:

> It is a serious question in my mind whether there should be individual homes for children – or even whether children should know their own parents ... If I were to offer to take any mother's child and guarantee it such an upbringing, and were even to convince the mother at the same time that she was unquestionably unfitted to bring up her child ... would she give up the child to me?

I can't imagine how vulnerable new mothers felt when reading Watson's advice. Can you?

Sir Frederic Truby King, or Truby King, as he was more

commonly known, a medical doctor from New Zealand, also spread messages which undoubtedly helped to undermine maternal instinct among new mothers. His aims were once again noble – I suspect he would be horrified if he realised the impact he had on a new mother's self-confidence and esteem. He was responsible for setting up the Plunket Society, formed to educate new mothers about the proper care of babies, covering feeding, health, hygiene and similar topics. The Plunket Society was incredibly effective in its goal to improve infant health and reduce mortality, and the organisation still exists today, under the new name of Plunket, remaining an important part of life in New Zealand, supporting around 85 per cent of new families and providing services for free.

Sadly, however, despite the important work King did in saving the lives of babies, he also helped to spread childist messages. In 1913, he published his book *Feeding and Care of Baby*, subtitled *To help the mothers and save the babies*.[6] Much of the book provided sound, practical advice for the safekeeping of babies, but when King strayed into advising on how to be a good mother and how to take care of babies emotionally, the book became childist: 'The "can't be so cruel" mother or nurse … who weakly gratifies every whim of herself and the child, rather than allow either to suffer temporary discomfort for the sake of permanent health and happiness – such a woman is really cruel, not kind.' Thankfully, Plunket, as an organisation, has moved on from King's theories, providing valuable support to families.[7] King's beliefs – those of spoiling babies with love, creating bad habits, and having to be cruel to be kind when disciplining children – still live on in society today, though.

Common belief: Children misbehave for attention, therefore we should ignore them when they are tantruming or similar, so we don't give them the attention they are looking for'

The idea of depriving children of attention to stop their difficult behaviour is taken a step further when a child is removed to 'time out', which involves standing or sitting them in a corner of a room, facing the wall, and demanding that they remain quiet and still for a set period of time. This punishment is meant to deter the child from behaving in an unwanted way again in the future.

Ignoring difficult behaviour can, once again, be traced back to the work of historical male childcare experts. In the 1980s, when he wrote his book, Green was a huge advocate of time out and separating children from their caregivers if they misbehave. If the child leaves the room before the time out is up, parents are instructed that 'a gentle smack should be administered before returning the child to his room, not so as to cause any pain, but merely to leave the child in no doubt that he is not welcome until better behaved'. Green believed that some toddlers could make themselves vomit on cue, as a further way to manipulate parents; if this happened, his advice was to remove the child to the bedroom, clean them up in a matter-of-fact way and return them straight back to their bedroom, without talking. After smacking a child, Green was most concerned that the mother should not crumble and cry or feel guilty. Similarly, the worst thing a mother could do after smacking her toddler was to cuddle them. Green said this taught toddlers to become more manipulative, inspiring further poor behaviour.

Removal of attention as a punishment to deter the child from repeating the same difficult behaviour in the future remains a theme common in much discipline advice today.

Common belief: Children should obey adults; harsh discipline is necessary to teach them respect

Many of the criticisms of gentle parenting (or at least what people *think* is gentle parenting) centre on the apparent lack of discipline: if gentle parenting respects children and doesn't utilise punishments as a form of discipline, then how are children taught to respect adults, ask detractors? In reality, harsh punishment can never teach respect; the only thing it can teach is fear. If children fear their parents and carers, then they are likely to obey temporarily – until such time as they are no longer scared. Similarly, they appear compliant initially, because they learn that they cannot be their authentic selves with their punisher. We will cover these ideas much more in Chapter 4. But where did the idea of hurting children to make them behave better come from? Sadly, it is one that has been around for ever, with many calling on religious texts, such as the Bible, to support their views. The hotly debated 'spare-the-rod, spoil-the-child' idea, from Proverbs, 13:24 is an example here ('Those who spare the rod hate their children, but those who love them are diligent to discipline them'), despite many Christians advocating for a far kinder interpretation.

One expert who agrees with the definition of 'sparing the rod' is the American Michael Pearl who, with his wife Debi, runs Bible study sessions and writes about disciplining children, with a religious leaning. Michael and Debi wrote their book *To Train up a Child* in 1994,[8] with sales of over 1.2 million copies worldwide since publication. Unsurprisingly, the book has a strong religious basis, regularly referring to Bible passages to back up claims. Indeed, the title of the book is taken from Proverbs, 22:6: 'Train up a child in the way he should go: and when he is old, he will not depart from it.' Like Watson's, the Pearls' advice is underpinned by the idea of conditioning fear into children to force them to behave in a desired way – a process referred to in the book as 'training'.

There is an undercurrent throughout the book that children are viewed as untrained and immoral, and that they must be trained to be good, obedient people by their parents.

The needs and rights of adults are considered above those of children in the book, the Pearls believing that children should obey if they want to be treated well by their parents, one passage stating:

> There is nothing cute or lovable about a whining 'brat.' To allow a child to whine and disobey is to mold a personality and character that you will eventually find hard to like. By taking control and teaching them to control their emotions and to instantly obey, your children will be cheerful and pleasant. Then you will not only love your children, but like them as well.

This viewpoint embodies childism and the discrimination of children.

It's no surprise to learn that the Pearls are advocates of physical forms of 'training', too. They are supporters of switching (hitting with an implement such as a wooden spoon, spatula or small, flexible willow branch), spanking and, for larger children, hitting with an implement such as a light belt. This is designed to bring about obedience and so-called respect, an idea that would not have been out of place a hundred years ago, echoing the fears conditioned into Little Albert by Watson.

Common belief: A good way to teach a child to not hurt others is to show them how it feels

Many believe that inflicting pain on a child to teach them to not inflict pain on others is a good way to discipline. This is certainly the school of thought followed by the Pearls when they advocate for spanking. Watson also believed that it was a good idea to inflict pain along with stern words when children displayed unwanted behaviour.

Discipline, according to Watson, was best done by fathers, as they were more scary and could elicit a greater fear response when a child displayed an unwanted behaviour. The cherry on the top of this fear-based discipline, was to incorporate physical pain by slapping a child's hand. According to Watson[9]:

> The slapping, or painful stimulus will make the child jerk back its hand. Again we have the stimulation at hand for setting up a conditioned negative response ... To get the right psychological conditions, the parent should always apply this painful stimulus just at the moment the undesirable act is taking place.

The newly conditioned fear was meant to steer the child away from repeating the behaviour in the future. Many still believe in a quick tap on the hand or biting back to control negative behaviours, and discipline through inflicting fear and pain remains sadly common almost a century after Watson's writings.

A time for change?

Although the work of the aforementioned childcare experts still underpins the way many adults interact with children today, more parents are beginning to shun their childist advice. Surprisingly, some of the experts themselves were also known to soften their views as they grew older and more experienced.

Christopher Green later completely reversed his opinions of raising children, something he claims was a result of a life-changing stroke, which left him with speech difficulties, and the death of his wife. In May 2007, in an interview with the

Australian radio station ABC Radio National, Green said: 'I used to be called the Toddler Tamer but I don't think we need to tame them any more – I think we really need to value them ... I think most behavioural problems are not problems if you can spend quality time with children and give them attention.' Richard Ferber also revised his book in 2006, softening his approach to tackling infant sleep issues.

Sadly, not all the experts have U-turned on their approach, perhaps because, as we will learn in Chapter 8, it is hard to consider that your views may be childist and to change them.

Regardless of changing expert opinions, the loudest voices in childcare today are often informed – subconsciously or otherwise – by the work of the original male childcare experts, and their childist methods are still the best known and most practised, continuing to influence millions of parents. (We will pick up on the childism in modern-day sleep training and discipline advice again in the following two chapters.) There are plenty of women who are willing to stand in their shoes, too, perpetuating their childist advice, albeit slightly watered down and phrased in a more palatable way, still focused on three main childist principles:

1. Adults having control over children
2. Leaving babies and toddlers to cry alone, to improve sleep and behaviour
3. Disciplining through shaming, punishment or exclusion.

You only have to read an article about childcare, switch on a television programme with a parenting segment or read a parenting discussion online to see these principles in action. These are the messages that have filtered down through generations and may be informing – whether consciously or unconsciously – your parenting today.

I think it's time we challenged them, don't you? But how?

We have to start by recognising the historical childism within mainstream parenting advice in the present. And that's exactly what we will do in the next two chapters, taking a deep dive into the sleep and discipline advice and childcare methods commonly recommended to parents today.

Chapter 3

The Childist Seeds of Yesteryear, Part One: Sleep

Fortunately, many parents still prefer to comfort their babies. If they didn't, we might find ourselves living in a society of very solitary people, who had learned to control their distress rather than to find strength through sharing it.

NAOMI STADLEN, psychotherapist and author

In the previous chapter, we considered the parenting advice and experts of yesteryear – those who have arguably been the most influential when it came to shaping childcare practices over the last century. As we have learned, two aspects come up repeatedly in current childcare practices today: sleep and discipline. For this reason, I have dedicated this chapter and the next to these areas, starting here with the childism inherent within the sleep-training methods common today.

The advice given to parents during the very earliest months and years of parenting sets the tone for the approaches recommended for the rest of their child's life. If we begin our parenting journey believing that we are somehow in battle with our child, and that as adults we need to win the fight for control, it is highly likely that this will colour interactions with our children for many years to follow. So, while I appreciate that you may (thankfully) be long past the exhausting sleepless-nights phase in your own life, I want, nevertheless, to take you back to the techniques and recommendations that are so often advocated to get babies and toddlers sleeping through the night, without night feeds and without human touch to settle them, both at bedtime and when they wake during the night. And if you are reading this with a bump, or a baby, or you care for children under the age of three professionally, then I hope this chapter will open your eyes to the childism behind the messages so often given – unsolicited – to tired new parents, and why they actually don't serve either parent or child. Ultimately, I hope to be able to help you to trust your instinct and respond to your child, or the children in your care, with the same respect you would hope to be afforded yourself should you be struggling with your own physical or psychological comfort at night. If you can recognise the childism that over-shadows interactions with your children in the earliest months of their lives, you will be well placed to recognise, and overcome, that which follows as they grow.

The inherent childism behind infant and toddler sleep training

Sleep training is a huge industry. Tired parents are sold a dream of a peacefully slumbering baby or toddler, if only they are prepared to work hard enough to achieve the goal. However, sleep training does both parent and child a disservice – the methods touted are often highly childist, disrespectful of the needs of babies and toddlers (namely, to maintain a close physical proximity with their primary caregiver, to receive adequate nutrition and to enable them to feel a state of calm and comfort both physically and emotionally), in the pursuit of meeting those of adults (to get a full night's sleep in order to be able to function well the next day).

Today's parents are undeniably exhausted, trying to raise babies with primitive needs, in a society that requires them to work as if they don't have any children and one where families are increasingly scattered geographically. There is no mythical supportive village and the increasing cost of living means parents need to focus on bringing in money to keep a roof over their heads and food on the table. Something has to give and, sadly, it is usually the children that bear the brunt.

Sometimes parents are duped (as I was) into believing that sleep training is the best thing for their child – that they must be strong enough to withstand the tears and pleas for cuddles and milk feeds in order to teach the valuable skill of self-soothing. Adverts and social media posts tell parents that sleep is something that has to be learned, and that they are responsible for teaching their children how to do it. And these tired parents are so heavily marketed to, and so shattered from burning the candle at both ends, trying to be a full-time parent, a full-time worker and keep the family home running, that they believe sleep training is the solution to their problems. It isn't.

Sleep-training messages, even those that purport to be gentle, perpetuate the situation desperate parents find themselves in, because nothing changes for the adults, and it is the demands on them that are, ultimately, the real cause of the struggles so many face. It's time for parents to become angry about sleep training (again, even that which is labelled gentle) because it erodes the rights of both adult and child. The more parents engage in talk about sleep training, employ sleep consultants or purchase products which promise peaceful slumber, the more they enable the inherent childism. And the longer this childism continues, disguising the real problems that parents face, the less likely politicians are to do something about it. Society is not supportive of tired parents with non-sleeping babies and toddlers because sleep training palliates the problem, temporarily hiding it. It's time to rip the band aid off: yes, it is likely that there will be pain in the short term, when shattered parents struggle with meeting the needs of their children and a full-time job or running a household, but ultimately, it is the only way that the insidious problem can be fully exposed and finally treated. Only when enough parents get angry about the impossible situations they find themselves in will they come together and campaign for better financial and practical support for young families.

When it comes to handling developmentally normal but undeniably taxing infant sleep, the solution so often touted is to reduce contact with the child, in order that they learn that crying does not result in the outcome they want or need. Much like the advice of the historical parenting experts outlined in the previous chapter, the primary guidance for tired parents centres on not creating bad habits, or breaking those already formed. A lot of blame is laid at the feet of parents; they are told that their children aren't sleeping because they are missing the signs of tiredness or have taught them to sleep only when they are fed or cuddled. They are told that their actions have prevented the all-important skill of self-soothing. Once again, this is rooted in the methods of historical childcare experts, who felt that they knew more than parents, overriding their instincts and causing them to question everything they felt to be right.

With all this in mind, let's look at some of the most popular sleep-training methods used today and consider the childism behind them.

Controlled crying

Controlled crying goes by many names: spaced soothing, graduated extinction, controlled comforting, rapid return, shushing and patting, pick up, put down – the list is almost endless. All these techniques are inspired by childist childcare history. They may have different names, but they are, ultimately, all the same because they all centre on delaying and reducing a parent's response to their child's needs. Sometimes parents are advised to leave the room and leave the child crying alone in their cot for a set period of time before returning (as is true for the practice most commonly known as controlled crying); sometimes the parents are allowed to stand next to their child's cot, but not pick them up (shushing and patting), or, if they are allowed to pick them up, they must put them down again as quickly as possible (pick up, put down).

Parents are taught to leave the child crying for increasing periods of time (with or without their presence in the room) in the belief that this will teach them to 'self-soothe' or 'self-settle'. However, this presumes that the child is capable of resolving any issues they are experiencing at the time. For instance, they are expected to soothe their own pain, resolve their own hunger and thirst, calm down any anxiety or fear they may have and fix any issues in the environment (room temperature, for example) that may be preventing sleep. But babies and toddlers just can't do these things independently. It is not possible for them to 'self-soothe' the myriad of physical and emotional problems that they are experiencing. What happens, therefore, when they do become quiet? Have they miraculously learned the skills required to solve all issues themselves? Or have they learned, through a process of conditioning (like Little Albert – see page 34), that their cries are in vain?

Interestingly, research shows that those babies who have been sleep trained with these methods do appear to sleep better initially (for 'sleep better' read they are quiet and cry less at night); however, in the long term, there is no improvement in their sleep compared to those babies who were never sleep trained.[1] Yet, if the sleep training did indeed help them learn to self-soothe, then surely, we would see a long-term benefit over their non sleep-trained peers? Not so. We also know from research that despite seeming to sleep better once trained, these babies are actually not getting any *more* sleep than their untrained peers, albeit their parents are likely getting more and mistakenly perceive their children's sleep to be improved, too.[2]

While the above research has shown that sleep training is, to all intents and purposes, pointless when it comes to long-term efficacy, it is harder to prove any harm (or, indeed, any absence of harm) scientifically. Research proving or disproving the harm of sleep training would require a colossal investment of both time and money. It would need to follow children into adulthood and consider all elements of their lives, including their physical and mental health, their relationships and more. Understandably, this is unlikely to ever happen, but without it, it is impossible to quantify the harm (or lack of it) that sleep training does to a child. Most of the research that does attempt to measure the impact of sleep training is highly flawed for one reason or another. Many studies focus on asking parents to assess any psychological harm caused by the techniques, which they are obviously unqualified to answer, plus they are biased towards believing no harm has come to their child. Some studies attempt to measure stress hormones secreted by babies when they are left to cry, but don't follow up on how this may, or may not, impact the child as they grow into adulthood. And other research relies on basic questionnaires and observations to study the potential psychological effects of sleep training – approaches that are far too simplistic to do the studies justice or uncover any true impact.

In my opinion, the biggest argument against sleep training is that it is totally at odds with normal childhood behaviour and infringes the rights of children for the sake of making life easier for adults.

If we question the morals of controlled crying, it is impossible to conclude that it doesn't involve an aspect of childism and prioritising the rights and needs of adults over children's.

Putting down awake/ avoiding feeding to sleep

There is much talk about 'bad habits', 'sleep props' and reliance on feeding and parental touch in the infant sleep-training world. Parents whose natural instincts are to rock and sway with their babies until they are sleeping or hold them in their arms long after they drift off are told that the secret to improving their child's sleep is to 'put them down in their cot drowsy but awake'. This sounds so simple, but it is anything but. Babies are not meant to be left to go to sleep independently; their instincts drive them to seek the safety and protection of their carers' arms. Their reflexes tell them that they are in danger when they sense themselves being put down in their cots and they naturally cry to be picked up again. Yet parents are advised to ignore their child's pleas and to sit next to the crib, 'shushing and patting', placing a hand on the baby, telling the child 'It's time to sleep now', or simply just smiling at them, unmoving. Sometimes the chair is moved further and further away from the cot, until the parent is sitting outside of the nursery, a method known simply as 'disappearing chair'. When these methods work, and the baby falls asleep, parents are meant to presume that the child can now 'self-soothe', a skill to be celebrated. However, for many parents in this situation, they feel far from triumphant. It can be brutal overriding your instincts while your baby is right next to you, desperate to be held. However, this method, popularised by historical childcare experts such as Truby King, continues to be the mainstay of modern-day sleep advice. As King said, 'disturbed sleep may be become habitual in a healthy baby if he is badly trained or spoiled, for instance by petting him whenever he wakes and cries, or worse still, by giving him food to stop crying'.

The same is true of avoiding feeding to sleep, be that breast- or bottle-feeding, the belief here being that feeding to sleep is a habit, or prop, that will cause issues with the baby connecting sleep cycles independently. They are said to 'wake for milk' more if they are fed to sleep, and the association must be broken. Much like trying to get a baby to go to sleep in his or her crib 'drowsy but awake', trying to prevent them falling asleep on the breast or bottle is a futile and frustrating task. You see, nature intended babies to fall asleep while feeding: breast milk contains hormones and enzymes that help to initiate sleep, the act of suckling on a bottle helps a baby to relax and the physical contact between parent and child encourages the release of oxytocin, the hormone of love, calm and safety. Falling asleep while feeding is the physiological norm for babies, and yet sleep-training advice makes it out to be problematic, meaning that tired, stressed and increasingly desperate parents attempt to break the natural link between feeding and sleep – something that is as distressing for their babies as it is for them.

Feeding schedules and night weaning

Have you ever considered how strange it is that adults get to decide when they are hungry and thirsty, eating and drinking according to sensations within their bodies, yet babies and toddlers are not trusted to know their own signals? They are fed formula milk according to the supposed amount recommended for their age, not their own unique hunger needs. Their night feeds are restricted, or ceased prematurely, when parents are advised to night wean, in order to improve sleep (in the mistaken belief that the night feeds are unnecessary habits). Even the NHS website states that babies over six months of age should no longer require milk at night. But who has asked the babies? While restricting night feeds for older babies may not cause them physical harm, providing of course that they are receiving enough nutrition in the daytime, it views the night-time needs of babies as inconsequential. Would we restrict milk in the daytime? If not, why is it OK to do so at night? Would we stop our partner from taking a drink of water to bed at night in case they woke with a dry throat? If not, why is it OK to do the same to babies? Why do we presume we know best for them and why do we once again prioritise our need for sleep over their need for food or drink? The moral questions behind this practice once again highlight the childism that underpins common advice, even that given by respected health authorities.

Sometimes parents are advised to 'fill children up' in the daytime to get them to sleep through the night. They are persuaded to load their children full of heavy foods in the run-up to bedtime, so that they won't need milk at night. While this may make sense in theory, the problem is that children are being encouraged to ignore their own hunger and satiety cues. If a child is not hungry, prompting them to eat more and more in a bid to keep them asleep at night can have long-term consequences, teaching them to overeat because they realise they make their parents happy when they eat a lot. Setting a child up, potentially, for an eating disorder is certainly childist, especially when it is rooted in prioritising adult sleep over the child following their instinctive drive to eat – or rather not eat.

Encouraging solo sleep

Isn't it strange that most adults choose to sleep next to their partner (if they have one) every night, yet we expect babies and toddlers to sleep alone, often in their own rooms. No other mammals put their young down overnight in their own, separate space – they all sleep in close contact with their babies. Modern-day humans, however, have decided that young children should be independent in their own rooms and beds as early as possible. Any desire to sleep with their parents, in the parental bed, is deemed problematic, and something that should be nipped in the bud as soon as possible.

If a toddler wakes in the night and dares to venture into their parents' bedroom, parents are advised to return them to their own room promptly, with as little interaction as possible. The fear here is that hugging the child, verbally reassuring or otherwise interacting with them may be perceived by the toddler as a reward for waking and leaving their room. Responding to toddlers who need you at night, however, is not remotely akin to rewarding them, nor does it perpetuate a problem. Toddlers do not have the brain development necessary to plot and scheme to wake at night to be 'rewarded' with attention from their parents. They wake because they have shorter sleep cycles than us, experience nightmares, fears and worries or physical discomfort, and don't have the ability to self-soothe. The insistence of the historical childcare experts and latter-day sleep trainers on forcing a young, vulnerable child to sleep alone is in direct conflict with their evolutionary need to be with their parents to feel safe.

What would we think if these sleep-training methods were used on vulnerable adults who were struggling to sleep at night? There would – rightly – be uproar if an elderly individual with dementia was left to cry or shut in their room alone with the equivalent of a baby gate preventing them from getting out if they needed help.

If it is not OK for adults, why is it OK for children?

In the many years I have been working with parents to help them understand their babies' and children's sleep patterns, I have found that the most effective approach to addressing the sleep deprivation that so often accompanies new parenthood is to focus on three areas:

1. Helping to develop a realistic view of what normal infant sleep looks like. If parents are aware that their child's sleep is normal (albeit exhausting), it is often much easier for them to cope with it.
2. Helping to uncover any potential issues that may be inhibiting the child from sleeping as well as can be expected developmentally. These issues can include trying to get the child to sleep more than they need, problems with lighting or temperature in the bedroom, or undiagnosed medical conditions.
3. Helping parents to consider small ways in which they can adjust their own lives to take off some pressure and allow more relaxation, so that they are better able to support their child's sleep needs temporarily (until the child grows and their night-time needs naturally lessen).

One family, who stick in my mind, came to me to ask for help with their baby's sleep. The baby was very fractious and hard to settle, even when the parents were as responsive and nurturing as possible. We tried a few tweaks to the environment and bedtime routine to no avail. Something didn't seem right and the baby was still very distressed, leaving the parents desperate to help. I suggested that they may want to consider visiting their family doctor in case there were any underlying physical reasons for the difficult sleep. A few months later, I received an email from the parents to let me know that their baby had been diagnosed with cancer. A tumour had been growing in the baby's stomach, causing great discomfort – and that discomfort was stopping the child from sleeping. Thankfully, treatment proved successful, the child recovered and naturally, their sleep improved. The parents expressed how grateful they were for not going through with the traditional sleep-training advice they had received from so many. Imagine what would have happened if that baby had been taught to no longer cry at night, and therefore no longer indicated their distress? It doesn't bear thinking about.

The sad reality is, as mentioned earlier, when sleep-training methods appear to work, they don't necessarily make the children sleep more, but just make them quiet, in much the same way that a Watsonian child learns to be quiet in time out. So, who exactly are these methods working for? Because it surely isn't the children. Sleep training doesn't meet their need for comfort, reassurance and connection at night, and it just palliates ours, by preventing us from demanding the change that we so desperately need to make family life easier. The root cause of our exhaustion isn't our children; it is the world we live in, the messages we are bombarded with and the fact that our society is not set up to meet the needs of parents of young children. The answer is not the unregulated trade of sleep training, selling expensive solutions based on fear and unrealistic promises, preying on the insecurities of shattered parents. If the childism at the heart of modern society's view of infant sleep and how to fix it was addressed, it would not only be good for our children but for us, too.

At this point I would like to pose three questions:

1. What are the underlying beliefs behind the sleep-training methods mentioned in this chapter? Do they seek to understand children and help to resolve underlying issues preventing them from sleeping in a desirable way? Or do they simply punish the children for having what adults perceive as a sleep problem?
2. Can you see a link between modern-day sleep-training methods and the teachings of historical childcare experts?

3. Would we deal with difficult sleep in an adult (say, an elderly resident in a care home) with the same methods? If not, why not?

Considering your answers to these questions, do you think modern-day sleep-training methods are childist? Do they show clear discrimination towards children and undermine their human rights?

I often refer to baby and toddler sleep-training advice as an epidemic. It seems that the prevalence of sleep consultants and their opinions and instructions works parents into a desperate frenzy, believing that their child has a problem that needs to be fixed and that the answer lies in expensive sleep solution packages and products. Add to this concern the exhaustion that accompanies night-time parenting in a society that does little to support parents to raise their children in the day-time, let alone at night, and sleep is soon pathologised, creating problems where there are none and convincing parents that the correct, and indeed sometimes only, thing to do is to put their own rights and needs above those of their children.

I have yet to meet a parent who honestly believes that leaving their child to cry at night is the right thing to do, but they follow the advice because that's what the experts recommend, even though (like me, when I tried it with my firstborn) it makes their heart sore. Desperate parents do not genuinely want to cause their children distress; they follow the methods because they feel there is nothing else they can do – and to do nothing would be catastrophic.

The question we should be asking here is what can we do to support both parent *and* child? How can we help both? And this is what I advocate for – an approach to infant and child sleep that is truly balanced, equitable and fair. I don't believe our society has fully embraced this idea yet, but I hope in the future it will.

Chapter 4

The Childist Seeds of Yesteryear, Part Two: Discipline

Man would indeed be in a poor way if he had to be restrained by fear of punishment and hope of reward.

ALBERT EINSTEIN, theoretical physicist

Much of the discipline advice today centres on ideas of creating 'good' children and teaching them to respect others. How many times have you heard somebody refer to a new baby saying, 'Oh, he's such a good boy; he rarely cries', or, when speaking to a toddler, 'Be a good girl; stop crying.'

The thing is, being 'good' here basically means the child hiding their emotions – and there is nothing good about that. And, sadly, the quest to encourage children to be quiet and compliant continues throughout the entirety of childhood, well into the teen years.

What makes a child 'good'? When I was a child, you were 'good' if you:

- slept all night in your own room (regardless of how scared or lonely you felt)
- ate all the food on your plate (even if you weren't hungry or didn't like it)

- did what adults told you to do without complaint (even if what they asked you to do felt wrong or too hard)
- didn't tantrum, sulk or whine (regardless of any big, difficult feelings)
- didn't interrupt adult conversation (however much you needed to)
- never answered back (no matter how important or valid your point)
- gave your relatives a hug or a kiss on demand (regardless of how uncomfortable you felt doing it).

What society really means by a child being 'good' is living inauthentically, keeping difficult emotions buried and hidden, overriding physical and psychological needs to please adults and imitating behaviour and neurological development beyond their years. The unspoken belief, therefore, is that a child who voices their needs or difficulties, requests help from those closest to them and who doesn't ignore their instincts or beliefs is 'naughty', 'difficult', 'rude' or 'disrespectful'.

We teach children, from birth, that we don't tolerate their crying very well – and we tolerate it even less as they grow older, with frequent complaints about tween and teen attitudes and stroppy moods appearing in Internet discussion forums. As a consequence, children learn to keep their difficult emotions in. We teach them to bury their feelings and that they can't trust us in their moment of need. And it is most definitely not 'good' to bury feelings, at any age.

What happens, then, when children become adults? Having spent years burying their feelings and not being able to trust anybody with them, the toxicity grows and it manifests in illness, addiction and relationship difficulties. Is it any wonder so many adults struggle with their mental health, eating and sleeping habits, and ability to uphold personal boundaries, instead falling into an unhealthy pattern of 'people pleasing'. We are trained into emotionally unhealthy behaviours from the very beginning of our lives.

The discipline techniques so often advocated today focus on establishing control and compliance to please adults, rarely considering the rights of children.

What does it mean when we talk about children respecting us? So many comments posted online in response to stories about children claim that 'kids need to learn respect these days', but children don't *learn* respect. Adults don't *teach* respect. Respect is something that we, as parents and caregivers, need to earn. Respect develops naturally when children are inspired, guided and supported by adults, when adults act with empathy and compassion. If you think of the people you respect most in your life, they are likely those who inspire you, who act with kindness, humility and good humour. Respect is absolutely, categorically never achieved through shaming, punishment, exclusion or guilt. The only things that develop here are disconnect and fear. If we want children to respect us, the solution is very simple: we have to start by respecting them.

Alas, as with sleep training, most discipline techniques today are still fixated on creating 'good' children and forcing respect, guided, yet again, by the childist beliefs of the historical male childcare experts and rarely considering how children feel, which is why they are problematic and ineffective as long-term solutions.

What do adults today think about disciplining children?

Almost all popular discipline techniques centre on the goal of trying to control children's behaviour by eliminating or supressing that which is undesirable to adults, even if the behaviour in question may be advantageous to the child's development. Most discipline techniques focus on trying to increase obedience and compliance.

Research has shown that adults grow more impatient when they become parents (understandably – it's exhausting work);[1] and what happens when we mix children with immature brains and a developmentally appropriate lack of impulse control and emotion regulation with tired, stressed, impatient adults? Most common discipline techniques are reactive in nature, focused on achieving a quick fix. They are usually coercive, trying to manipulate a child's behaviour through the use of carrots (rewards and praise) and sticks (shaming, yelling, exclusion and punishments). These reactive discipline techniques all lack a deeper understanding of a child's needs and struggles, failing to uncover the cause of their tricky behaviour and work with them to resolve the underlying problem. Such superficial approaches mean that the cause of the difficult behaviour remains hidden, ready to grow and become something much harder to handle in the future.

If we seek to discipline with carrots and sticks, we may temporarily see an obedient child, one who is too scared to cry or release their emotions for fear of punishment or losing promised rewards. However, the initial problems remain unsolved, and because the child knows that they cannot rely on their parents or carers to help them, they learn to override their feelings, believing that they are only lovable when they are placid and calm. They learn to put the needs of others first, to conceal their feelings so that their parents are happier and calmer.

A lack of connection between adult and child in the moment of struggle means that children are often left alone at times of vulnerability and their highest need. So, when they are grappling with something that causes them to be emotionally dysregulated, leaving them alone with their dysregulation (or what adults commonly term as 'naughty behaviour') does not teach them to calm down; instead, it teaches them that they can't trust us when they're struggling, and it leaves them lacking in emotion-regulation skills as they grow – because these are the skills they learn from us when we comfort them. In turn, we unwittingly raise them to perpetuate the cycle when they become adults and care for children of their own.

This pattern can impact relationships as children grow and they become at risk of developing externalising behaviours (where the big feelings are manifested as anger and violence towards others) or internalising behaviours (where the feelings are drawn further inwards and can manifest as anxiety, low self-esteem and self-destructive behaviours, such as alcoholism, drug abuse and self-harm). I don't believe any parent or carer sets out for any of this to happen when they discipline their children, yet the childist undercurrent of today's techniques dupes them into believing that being harsh is the best way and that they have to be cruel to be kind. There is a constant misguided pursuit of respect in society today, where the belief is that if adults control and rule through fear, children will respect them.

Let's take a look at some common methods parents and carers are using to discipline children of all ages today. As you read through them, consider the work of the historical parenting experts we looked at earlier and how their influence still sets the tone.

Punishments/consequences

This stick-based approach builds on Watson's conditioning work, the idea being that if a child is punished for a specific behaviour, they will be less likely to repeat it in the future because they will remember the negative consequences of their actions. Very often, adults punish children for behaviour without forethought; they just feel that the behaviour deserves a consequence, usually because they themselves would have received one for the same behaviour as a child.

Consequences can be a helpful tool for children to learn if they are natural – i.e. what happens naturally in response to their action, with no input from anybody else. For instance, if a child puts a favourite book into a bath full of water, the book will be ruined, making it unreadable. Ultimately, it is natural consequences that teach children about life and how to make sense of and control their own actions as they grow. There is another type of consequence that can help older children to learn; known as logical consequences, these can teach children how to put things right when they make a mistake if they are put in place in collaboration with the supervising adult. For instance, if a child reaches for a forbidden item out of reach in a kitchen cupboard, then accidentally drops it and creates a mess on the kitchen floor, the logical consequence is that they would either clear up the mess alone (if it is safe) or help the adult to do so (if adult input is required).

Most consequences used as a form of discipline, however, are poor teachers because they are usually illogical. Illogical consequences are simply punishments, often dished out by stressed, angry, impatient adults. They do not teach the child anything about their behaviour (or how they can do better next time) because they have no logical link to it – for instance, telling a child that because of their behaviour, they cannot go to their friend's house tomorrow, as promised.

A study of over 2,000 parents of toddlers found that 65 per cent regularly employed consequences to punish poor behaviour, most commonly removing a favourite toy or a treat.[2] Removal of a toy or treat is almost always an illogical consequence. The only time this would be logical is if the toy being removed was taken away to ensure the safety of another person or object. Banning a child from their computer, tablet, gaming system and similar again falls into the illogical-consequence category. There is no difference between punishment and illogical consequences; both are ineffective (in the long term) and constitute childist forms of discipline.

Yelling/shouting

All parents yell at their children at times. The perfect parent does not exist. Here, I'm not talking about the times when you try your hardest, but for whatever reason, your temper frays and you explode at your children. I'm talking about something quite different: choosing to yell, or shout at children consciously, as a form of discipline – something that is often referred to as 'fear-of-God' (or FOG) parenting. The goal here is simple: the adult shouts and makes themselves seem as intimidating as possible, in an attempt to scare the child into submission. When questioned, 60 per cent of parents of toddlers admitted to consciously shouting at their children as a form of discipline and the older the child, the more likely parents were to yell at them.[3]

In the teen years, yelling often becomes the 'go-to' first-line discipline approach, because parents don't know what else to do. Teenagers are much harder to control than younger children. Parents and carers are no longer able to manipulate their teens' behaviour with stickers, rewards or other inexpensive bribes, and now the child rivals them for physical size, they can no longer be controlled physically either. Simply, when the fear and lure of rewards disappear, parents are left with nothing discipline wise. Children are not compliant or easy to coerce into better behaviour when they are not scared. Yelling and shouting can damage the parent–child relationship to such an extent that teenagers show little respect for their parents because they, in turn, do not feel respected. Respect always has to be mutual to help with discipline. A relationship lacking connection and respect can quickly become toxic; add to that the loss of control due to a lack of fear, and the teen years can become incredibly hard for both parent and child. Finally, a child who has been raised by parents who yell when the going gets tough will often grow to become an adult who yells and shouts to resolve conflict. After all, if it was good enough for their parents, it's good enough for them.

Time out

Time out is not new; it has been advocated as a form of discipline for over a century. Again, the idea behind the process is another form of conditioning, based on Watson's original work (see page 35), whereby if the child misbehaves or does something the parent or carer is unhappy with, they are removed from the company of the adult and sent to a specific area where they are to sit, or stand, quietly, until the adult allows them to leave. While in time out, the child is supposed to think about their actions, the impact they had on others and what they could do better next time, the length of the time out being supposedly appropriate to their age (the older the child, the longer the time out). In reality, the child most likely does not think about any of these things; what they do learn, however, is that in their moments of greatest need (when their overwhelming emotions mean that they cannot control their behaviour) their parents and carers are not there for them. They learn to be quiet to be allowed out of time out and appease their parents. They learn to mask their feelings and act in ways that others prefer. Time out is a perennial favourite of parenting courses, including those professing to be positive in nature, and is often recommended by health professionals when parents seek advice for difficult behaviour. When questioned, 70 per cent of parents of toddlers said that they regularly used time out as a form of discipline.[4]

What children really need when they are struggling with their behaviour is adults who are calm and supportive and can help them learn to regulate their emotions. They need adults to stay with them, to teach them better ways to behave and manage situations – adults who take time to understand what has caused the problem in the first place, so that it can be resolved. Sadly, none of this happens when a child is put in time out, they are simply left to deal with their problem alone.

The naughty step

The naughty step is simply another version of time out. Instead of being sent to a corner of the room, or into another room entirely (a favoured location of time out), the child is sent to sit on a designated naughty step. The naughty step is a technique first popularised by childcare author Jo Frost (more commonly known as Supernanny), who, in her 2011 book *Jo Frost's Confident Toddler Care: The Ultimate Guide to the Toddler Years* described it as 'a very effective and efficient way to teach a child that some behaviour is not acceptable'[5].

Advocates of the naughty step technique commonly recommended that when children misbehave they are first warned to stop the unwanted behaviour otherwise they will be taken to the naughty step. If this warning doesn't work, the parent should then take the child to the naughty step, make them sit down and remain sitting, quietly, for one minute for each year of their life (a two-year-old would remain for two minutes and so on). If the child does not remain on the step for the specified period of time then they should be returned and the timer reset. If the child cries out while on the step, parents are to ignore their pleas.

Distraction

Distraction is commonly recommended to parents as an effective way to discipline, the idea being that if a child's behaviour is difficult, then redirecting their attention to something interesting should end the behaviour. The NHS website advises the use of distraction as a method to manage toddler tantrums, stating, 'If you think your child is starting a tantrum, find something to distract them with straight away. This could be something you can see out of the window. For example, you could say, "Look! A cat." Make yourself sound as surprised and interested as you can.'[6]

Initially, distraction appears to be a more positive discipline technique, however it still does not solve the underlying emotions or problem that is causing the child's difficult behaviour; in fact, it could, arguably, make them worse. What happens if a child is struggling, and rather than asking them how they are feeling and seeking to help them, we gloss over their emotions or ignore them, instead distracting them with something? What are we teaching them? That we don't want to deal with them when they're struggling? That we can't handle their emotions? How do you feel as an adult if someone attempts to change the subject (a form of distraction) when you are opening up about your feelings?

Instead, ideally, the adult will be strong enough emotionally to sit with the child and metaphorically 'hold' their big feelings, allowing them to release them in order to reach a resolution and state of emotional homeostasis. Only this approach will allow a child to release pent-up emotions and help to uncover the potential causes and triggers behind them.

Ignoring the child

Ignoring children when they misbehave is common advice. It presumes that children misbehave for attention, and that if they are starved of it, we will extinguish the unwanted behaviour. In a survey of 1,000 Scottish parents, 52 per cent said that they ignored their child when they were having a tantrum.[7] Is ignoring difficult behaviour really an effective form of discipline, though? How does it help a child who is struggling with something? And what about the child who is feeling disconnected from their parent or carer and who desperately needs physical touch, and emotional connection in order to feel more secure? What do we teach them when we ignore their cries for attention (and for attention, read connection)?

Very simply, adults need to meet a child's need for attention. If children are struggling because they feel disconnected to us and their behaviour is a desperate bid for our attention, it makes much more sense to recognise this need and take some time to reconnect with them. Only when children feel connected, seen and heard by the adults who care for them do they grow to feel worthy, to trust others and to develop good self-esteem. And when a child feels better, they behave better.

Rewarding/praising good behaviour

So far, we have focused on the 'sticks' of discipline, but what of the carrots? Ninety-nine per cent of parents questioned said that they had used praise as a form of discipline with their children, while 91 per cent used rewards when children were well behaved to encourage a future repeat of the positive behaviour.[8]

It feels good as an adult to give a child a sticker or a sweet if they have behaved 'well', so surely it feels good for the child, too? Rewards usually produce quick, but temporary results. This is because they do not deal with the cause of the issue. They don't rectify the problem or resolve the difficult feelings underlying the behaviour; they just temporarily coerce a desired behaviour while the child is fixated on the reward on offer.

The biggest misconception about behaviour when using rewards is that the child can control and change it. Rewarding as a discipline method presumes that the problem is not ability, but rather motivation. Only this isn't true; it's usually the very opposite and therefore a method focusing solely on motivation, disregarding ability, will always be ineffective. Rewards work on increasing extrinsic (external) motivation, but any positive effects are very superficial. For real change to take place we need to work with a child's intrinsic (internal) motivation, which, unfortunately, is damaged by the use of rewards. But the child is not learning 'right from wrong' or becoming a better person when you use rewards; instead, they comply while the reward is on offer, but when you remove the reward (or offer one that doesn't tempt them enough), you lose their compliance.

Maybe one of the saddest aspects of relying on rewards as a discipline strategy is that when children are unable to control their behaviour for whatever reason, they effectively end up punished by the lack of reward. A child who is struggling to behave because they are going through a difficult situation, or one who struggles to behave in expected ways because they have ADHD, or similar, can end up feeling quickly demoralised and demotivated, when they fail to receive rewards, especially if their siblings or classmates receive them. If 91 per cent of parents regularly use rewards as a form of discipline, that means there are a lot of children struggling when they don't receive a reward, usually through no fault of their own.

Once again, the answer is to help the child with any problems that are underpinning their difficult behaviour. If we work collaboratively with the child to ensure all their physical and emotional needs are met, as well as trying to reach a resolution to anything that is causing them discomfort, then – and only then – we can expect their behaviour to change. Similarly, working on our connection with children, so that they want to help us, for no reason other than it feels good to do so, is far more likely to create a helpful child than any form of coercion or behaviour control.

At this point, I would like to pose three questions:

1. What are the underlying beliefs behind all the methods mentioned so far in this chapter? Do they seek to understand children and help to resolve underlying

issues preventing them from behaving 'well'? Or do they simply punish the children for having a problem? Or try to coerce them into hiding their feelings?

2. The discipline advice from the historical childcare experts focused very much on controlling children through making them feel fear when they misbehaved. Can you see a link between these teachings and modern-day discipline techniques

3. Would we deal with poor behaviour from an adult with the same methods? If not, why not?

Considering your answers to these three questions, do you think common discipline techniques used today are childist? Do they show clear discrimination towards children and undermine their human rights?

Nobody really smacks children any more, do they?

One form of discipline we haven't discussed so far in this chapter, is corporal punishment, or punishment involving physical violence, such as smacking, spanking and similar. Whenever I give talks to parents about discipline, and ask if they were smacked by their parents as children, at least three quarters raise their hands. I then ask them if they believe smacking is still common in society today, and usually only one or two raise their hands. A 2021 YouGov poll of 3,000 adults in the UK found that 32 per cent believed smacking to be a good form of discipline.[9] The same poll found that 83 per cent of all respondents said that they themselves were smacked at least once by their own parents when they were children, with 11 per cent admitting that they were hit often. Research from Australia, found that 61 per cent of Australian teens said that they had been smacked at least three times by their parents. While the incidence of smacking and spanking is noticeably decreasing, thanks, in part, to bans such as those imposed by Scotland and Wales (see page 22 in Chapter 1), it is likely that the true percentage of parents who hit their children is higher than these surveys and polls find;[10] many parents will feel uncomfortable admitting that they do sometimes hit their children and therefore be reluctant to report their actions either via an online poll or, even less likely, to a researcher in person.

In the USA, spanking is more common than it is in the UK, with 45 per cent of children under the age of nine having been spanked in 2022.[11] The American Academy of Pediatrics (AAP), however, opposes spanking, formally stating: 'The AAP recommends that adults caring for children use healthy forms of discipline, such as positive reinforcement of appropriate behaviors, setting limits, redirecting, and setting future expectations. The AAP recommends that parents do not use spanking, hitting, slapping, threatening, insulting, humiliating, or shaming.'[12] Yet, despite this firm stance, up to 20 per cent of American paediatricians still support spanking children, with male doctors being much more likely to endorse it than females.[13]

Research has repeatedly found smacking children to be a poor form of discipline. It is ineffective at positively changing behaviour over the long term and comes with many risks. A recent meta-analysis of research from around the world, covering over 160,000 children, highlighted this, showing that children who were disciplined using physical punishment were more likely to develop mental-health issues and display antisocial behaviour in the long term.[14]

Given the lack of efficacy and potential harm, therefore, why do parents today continue to smack and spank their children? For many, it is an unconscious reaction, a hangover from their own childhoods, which we'll discuss much more in Chapter 8.

Another reason is that harsh discipline, such as physical punishment, can help adults to feel a sense of power and can also act as a release for their own pent-up stress and emotions. This, in turn, helps them to feel better about the situation and themselves because difficult behaviour from children can leave adults feeling out of control, and when they smack their children it restores that sense of control and balance of power back to them. Finally, hitting a child initially seems to work well, in the sense that it usually stops the unwanted behaviour in its tracks. This positive feedback can cause parents to believe that smacking is effective and thus repeat it again in the future.

The following quote, from child psychologist and psychotherapist Haim Ginott, perfectly describes the discrimination and childism at the heart of physically disciplining children:

> When a child hits a child, we call it aggression.
> When a child hits an adult, we call it hostility.
> When an adult hits an adult, we call it assault.
> When an adult hits a child, we call it discipline.

If child rights are human rights, why is it children are the only humans we are still legally allowed to hit in many countries?

'But we need to prepare them for the harsh world of adulthood'

I can't tell you how often I hear this in reply to articles I share online. I can guarantee that within the first hour of posting, at least one person will pop up and reply, 'That's all well and good, but they've got to learn – the adult world is tough'.

I recently shared a video I had filmed discussing the idea of allowing children to have 'mental-health days' a handful of times per year. The idea here is to allow children to stay at home (providing there is an adult there to care for them – something not possible for all families, I appreciate) and miss school in order to catch up on some much-needed rest and recuperation. I discussed that I had allowed my own children to take time off when they were exhausted, feeling run down or just needed a day to hibernate under a duvet, and that I restricted this to only once per school term. I commented that mental health was no different to physical health and that I believed we should treat them equally when it came to allowing children time to recover at home. This video quickly became one of the most controversial I have ever shared. Replies quickly came in saying, 'Children today need to toughen up!' 'I can't take a day off work if I'm tired – why should children be entitled to?' 'We're raising a generation of snowflakes; they're going to have a shock when they're adults!' and, 'They need to learn to suck it up and get ready for the real world.' Others argued that allowing children a rare day at home, when it was most needed would make teachers' jobs harder – although many teachers replied that when they're exhausted and feeling down, children can be harder to teach, and that a one-day reset could make a tangible difference to classroom life. The real issue with my suggestion was that it triggered many adults, whose own needs in childhood were not met, or their emotions valued and heard, and they grew to believe that other children deserve the same treatment. We will discuss the idea of 'the stiff upper lip' later (in Chapter 8) and how the cycle of childism, from generation to generation, is behind these beliefs.

We must also ask: why do we feel the need to be harsh to children today in a misguided attempt to prepare them to better cope with the adult world? They are not adults; they have no need to be thrown prematurely into the harsh world that we live in. Why don't we focus on nurturing them now, so that they develop better emotion-regulation skills to cope with life when they are older? Or why don't we focus on nurturing them now, so that their generation may be the one to change the harshness of our world in the future?

Why most school discipline is childist

Please note, that when I discuss the issues of school discipline here, I am not blaming teachers or anybody else who works in a school. The blame lays solely at the feet of politicians. (In Chapter 5, we will talk about what I call 'state-sponsored childism', or the childism so blatantly shown by governments, affecting all aspects of children's lives, including their education, especially in the UK.) Teachers are doing their best in a broken system. That broken system has, however, resulted in many childist discipline policies being implemented in schools because of the need to control huge class sizes, with inadequate SEND (special educational needs and disabilities) and pastoral support, while teaching an ever-changing curriculum in a system obsessed with educational-outcome metrics. Teachers are as much victims of the system as children (again, something we will discuss more in Chapter 5). They deserve our understanding and empathy, not our ire.

Arguably schools – the places that should be most geared towards the needs of children – have become some of the most childist institutions because they have been forced to adopt childist discipline policies as a quick fix for a broken system. It is common for schools today to adopt an authoritarian approach to difficult behaviour (see Chapter 8), focused heavily on carrots and sticks, punishing children who dare to step out of line. In the UK, the so-called government 'behaviour tsar', Tom Bennett, has helped to shape behaviour policies in schools and is credited for the zero-tolerance approach adopted by so many, embracing the full array of school-based punishments (which he terms 'sanctions'), as discussed later in this section, as well as rewards, praise and awards, all designed to make children more compliant and obedient at school. In 2017, Bennett conducted a review of behaviour in schools for the UK government.[15] His review often refers to 'successful schools' – those topping the league tables regularly – and implies that a zero-tolerance approach to behaviour is key to those schools' success. There is little mention of the children who are failed by their schools, those 'repeat offenders' who are excluded, leave for a different school with a more holistic approach to behaviour or drop out and disengage with the education system entirely. The omission of these children from reports and results tables can indeed make a school seem more successful, but for whom? Certainly not the children who have been failed by this discipline approach.

Let's look at some of the common discipline techniques used in schools today. As we work through them, consider how they mirror the advice given to parents by the historical childcare experts – those with an emphasis on adults having control over children and externally manipulating behaviour through fear-based punishment and/or the presence or absence of rewards and bribes. It is no coincidence that school-based discipline is very similar to that most commonly advised to parents, given that its roots remain firmly focused on outdated, childist principles.

Sending the child out of the classroom

A common technique employed with younger school children is sending them to wait outside the classroom, to a different class or to the headteacher. This works in the same way as time out (see page 68) – by removing children from their peers, with an added element of embarrassment and of fear (having to visit the headteacher).

Sad clouds and traffic-light systems

Once again, a technique usually reserved for younger children, this involves them missing out on class treats, play time and other special events. The charts are used as a visual tool to remind children to 'do better' and also to display their poor behaviour for their classmates to see, presuming that a child will feel ashamed if they are the only one on the sad cloud or red traffic light (the place where the 'naughty' children's names sit). The idea here is that children will aim to avoid the 'naughty' sections and instead be inspired to behave better to get a treat, like their classmates. The problem arises when they are unable to change their behaviour, perhaps because of SEND or another issue they are struggling with, and they end up almost permanently on the sad cloud or red traffic light.

Detentions

As children reach adolescence, there is a big shift in school discipline policies, with more of a focus on punishments or 'sanctions'. If a child misbehaves, the punishment usually involves them missing their free time, either their lunch break or time after school. Instead, they are kept inside for a detention, where they are usually required to write lines (yes, that still exists), do their homework, read a book (a fine way to make children dislike reading) or complete a special detention task. Once the time is up, the child is allowed to leave, the assumption being that the experience will prevent them from behaving poorly in the future. In reality, most detention rooms are full of the same children, repeat offenders who quickly get used to having no lunch breaks or free time after school. Ironically, these are usually the children who desperately need time outside to let off steam to be able to concentrate more in lessons.

Isolation booths and rooms

Isolation booths or rooms are one step up from detentions. Again, they work on the behaviourist principle of punishing a child for their behaviour and are often justified as keeping other pupils safe in the offending child's absence. They require the child to sit in isolation from their peers for a set period of time, usually a morning or afternoon, or sometimes the whole day. On Twitter, Tom Bennett stated that he believed renaming isolation will help to improve the reputation of the technique, saying, 'If you called them "removal rooms" then people would be far less upset about them. "Isolation rooms" sound like solitary in Sing-Sing.'[16] It is not the name that is the issue, however, but the concept behind it.

What about working with the child to uncover the causes behind the behaviour? For instance, a child who is intent on verbally abusing and humiliating others may well be one who is being bullied or abused at home. Similarly, there is little about re-educating the child, helping them to realise why their behaviour is so damaging and teaching them better ways to behave; instead – in a very Watsonian way – children are removed from their peers and placed in time out and then some, the presumption being that if the punishment is severe enough, as with Little Albert (see page 34), it will condition their behaviour and prevent a repeat. Only it doesn't work, as proven by the fact that the same children are seen in isolation again and again and again. One recent review of school discipline policies with a specific focus on isolation found no significant improvement in behaviour since the introduction of tougher policies, this despite an increase in sanctions given out.[17] One child questioned for the review explained the feeling of being put into isolation, saying, 'I can't put into words what you felt like, almost a dog in a cage.'

Interestingly, Bennett denies that isolation is childist, stating, 'Nobody's human rights are being interfered with'. However, the only time adults are placed in 'removal rooms' is when they are being held by the police on suspicion of a crime or when they are found guilty and imprisoned. Despite Bennett's protestations, it seems that human rights are indeed being infringed here for children.

School exclusions

The next step up the punishment or sanction chain is school exclusion, where the child is removed from the school either temporarily (for a day or a week, say) or permanently. Exclusions are supposed to act as a deterrent, but it is usually the children who struggle the most who find themselves excluded – for instance, those with a negligent or abusive parent at home or those who have been diagnosed as having special educational needs. These children often leave the education system entirely and their lack of qualifications can cause them to enter a life of unemployment or poverty as a result.

Behaviour-related school exclusions are on the rise – a worrying trend given the lack of evidence to show an improvement in behaviour.[18] There is, however, evidence showing a clear link between children who were repeatedly excluded at school and an increased risk of them committing crime. Research looking into the education history of young offenders between the ages of fifteen and eighteen has found that 86 per cent of them were excluded from school.[19] It is clear that these sanctions are failing the most vulnerable children in society, while neglecting to improve the education experience for others.

Individual merits, certificates and awards

On the 'carrots' side of the behaviour-control pendulum sit praise and rewards. These often take the shape of merit and headteacher certificates, stickers and awards. Sometimes the child will be called to receive their award in assembly or special awards evenings may be arranged.

The issue with using rewards at schools is the same as with parents using them at home. The effects are superficial and children who are struggling will often feel left out through their lack of reward. They are often the ones who desperately need help and attention, yet it is their more fortunate classmates who are recognised.

Class points

In the earlier years of school, behaviour is often modified using a class points-based system. The idea here is that the children work together to behave well and are rewarded, as a class, for their efforts. While this sounds good in theory, what of those children who struggle to behave and let the team down? Maybe they could be spurred on to better behaviour by their peers, but if they are struggling, this could quickly lead to peer shaming and isolation.

Attendance awards

While not a discipline technique, special mention must be given to attendance awards: as pressure builds on schools to increase pupil attendance, more and more are introducing these to encourage children into school when they are feeling sick, exhausted and in need of a mental-health day. While the idea is obviously aimed at those children with consistently poor attendance, it is unlikely to improve their attendance as much as the 'general population' of school. Children with chronically low attendance will often have medical conditions requiring time off school, some will struggle to be in the school setting because of mental-health reasons and others because of the issues of their parents. It is unjust that these children are effectively punished (through the lack of awards) for something that is almost always out of their control. It is not uncommon for secondary schools to hold termly raffles to win iPads and the like to encourage teenagers to attend school. The promotion of attendance awards is often lauded by those who believe that children should be more resilient, 'suck it up' and go to school regardless of how they feel (those with the same opinions demonstrated in the uproar that followed my video encouraging parents to allow their children to take a day off when they are feeling low – see page 75).

Toilet restrictions

Another non-discipline-related childist act that occurs at most schools is the restriction placed on children visiting the toilet during class time. They are encouraged to visit the toilet during breaks and lunchtime and are denied access during lessons. Some schools have even gone so far as to police the toilet entrances or install gates that remain locked during lesson times. Understandably, children visiting the toilet can be disruptive to lessons and there will always be those who take advantage and pretend to need the toilet in order to skip lessons – however, the majority are honest and genuine in their need.

Secondary schools often require students to use the toilet in between lessons, yet the sheer size of some schools and the five or ten minutes sometimes needed to get from one end of the school to the other for lessons can mean there is insufficient time to use the toilet, especially taking into consideration that there may be queues for a relatively small number of toilet blocks. Children can therefore find themselves joining a new lesson desperately needing the toilet, but unable to go for another hour or two, until the next break time. I have heard horrifying stories of young children wetting or soiling themselves in front of their peers when their request to visit the toilet was denied. What impact does this have on them when their peers laugh and tease them for their lack of control? Similarly, tween and teen girls are unfairly punished when they need to change towels, tampons, cups and period pants mid-lesson, and find themselves leaking on to their clothing or chair when they are denied.

Some schools have formulated a workaround to the menstruation issue by giving girls red cards or similar to show when they are on their period. The idea here is that when they announce to the whole class, by showing their red card, that they are currently menstruating, they are allowed to visit the toilet. Of course, the very fact that the whole class is now aware of their menstrual cycle and the embarrassment that this brings is dismissed. On a similar note, one of my children has coeliac disease, and would often find himself accidentally 'glutened', resulting in severe diarrhoea. After a few occurrences of being denied access to the toilet during lesson time, I spoke with the school and they issued him with a 'toilet pass'. If he found himself needing the toilet during class he was to hold up his pass and show the teacher, who would allow him to go to the toilet, no questions asked. However, this caused him huge levels of anxiety when he did not want to explain to the thirty other children in the class what was wrong with him and why he could not control his bowels. He would, instead, often ring me in tears and ask me to collect him, so that he could go to the toilet in privacy at home.

Can you imagine if adult workplaces had similar restrictions? How would you feel if you desperately needed to visit the toilet during a meeting, and instead of quietly excusing yourself, you had to hold up a bright red card advertising to your colleagues that you were menstruating or a pass indicating that you found it hard to control your anal sphincter? Yes, a class full of children needing to go to the toilet is frustrating and distracting; however, depriving them of a human right to privacy and meeting the needs of their most basic bodily functions is surely far worse?

As we close this section on school behaviour control, I would like to pose three questions:

1. Article 28 of the UN Convention on the Rights of the Child states: 'Parties shall take all appropriate measures to ensure that school discipline is administered in a manner consistent with the child's human dignity and in conformity with the present Convention'. Do you believe that isolation booths treat children with human dignity? Or are they in contravention with this code?
2. Article 31 of the UN Convention on the Rights of the Child states: 'Parties recognize the right of the child to rest and leisure, to engage in play and recreational activities appropriate to the age of the child and to participate freely in cultural life and the arts'. Do you believe that lunchtime detentions are in contravention of this code?
3. If our education system requires teachers to use the behavioural-control methods outlined here as a form of crowd control, because they cannot give the individual attention needed to discipline in a more respectful way, is our education system childist?

Childist approaches to discipline, whether at home or at school, all have one thing in common: they blame children for having a problem and not being able to resolve it independently. This echoes the common approaches to sleep training that we examined in the previous chapter. Once again, techniques to tackle the so-called 'behaviour problem' do nothing to help a child to resolve their problems, nor do they uncover the root cause of their difficulties with regulating their behaviour; they simply punish the child when their behaviour is not up to adult standards, whether with harsh consequences, removing the child from their friends and family or by withdrawing a reward that was previously on offer if they were 'good'.

Each of these techniques is informed by the male childcare experts of history, with a focus on adults being in control and behaviour manipulated with coercion. They do not instil respect; at best, they create fear and anxiety – yet once a child has become accustomed to the unjust treatment or is no longer scared of the disciplining adult, all control is lost. Then behaviour often worsens, and the one hope to improve behaviour and outcomes for the child – the relationship between child and carer – is lost, sometimes irrevocably.

These techniques all position the rights of adults above those of children, treating children in ways that we would usually only reserve for incarcerated adults who commit crimes. Childism is rife today when it comes to discipline in the places where children should be at their safest and most supported: at home and at school. For the sake of our children, and those who follow, we must draw attention to childist beliefs and actions, and consign them firmly back to the past, where they belong. We must also question the authorities allowing these techniques to be used, encouraging them, even, in state-sponsored institutions such as schools. This failure to act to prevent childism at a governmental level is something we will consider in the next chapter.

Chapter 5

State-sponsored Childism

Taking care of children has nothing to do with politics. I think perhaps with time, instead of there being a politicisation of humanitarian aid, there will be a humanisation of politics.

AUDREY HEPBURN,
actor and humanitarian

As Audrey Hepburn said, taking care of children should have nothing to do with politics, yet politics are responsible, directly or otherwise, for almost all childism that exists in the world today. Our politicians are the ones who shape public policy, fund children's services, education and healthcare and control our benefits system. Politicians are responsible for the economic climate that shapes the experience of parenting and influences decisions made by families. Politicians, ultimately, have control over almost every element of a child's life.

Childism doesn't only exist in the home, although it begins there, and everybody has been affected by it, including those at the highest levels of office. If adults grow believing that children are not worthy of the same degree of respect as they are, then any policies they form will reflect this. Childism on an individual level therefore links to childism on an institutional level, only here we are not talking about the treatment of an individual child – we are talking about the treatment of *all* children. And as long as children continue to be discriminated against in politics, politicians will keep making decisions that do not value them, their families or their carers, and so the cycle of childism perpetuates, which only makes things harder for individual children and their parents.

When launching her Shaping Us campaign in early 2023, the Princess of Wales gave a speech, saying:

> The campaign is fundamentally about shining a spotlight on the critical importance of early childhood and how it shapes the adults we become ... This is why it is essential to not only understand the unique importance of our earliest years, but to know what we can all do to help raise future generations of happy, healthy adults.

She went on to say, 'Those involved in raising children today need the very best information and support in helping to achieve this mission. And this campaign aims to help do that too.' These aims are admirable; however, we don't need more awareness about the importance of early childhood or more information aimed at parents. These have existed for decades already. What we really need is better funding of public services, action to reduce poverty, proper investment in the childcare system and governments that genuinely care about children and their families. Until this happens, awareness and information are merely a sticking plaster over a wound that will continue to fester and severely limit the impact of any campaigns aimed at improving the lives of children.

While this chapter mainly considers the effects of state-sponsored childism in the UK, the same principles apply to almost every country. Some are better in some respects and some are worse, yet all are inherently childist at the core. If you are not from the UK, I urge you to research similar issues in your own home country and pinpoint the inherent childism so that you are equipped to call it out where you find it.

Introducing the problem of neoliberalism

Neoliberalism is a huge source of fuel for childism today and it is so entrenched in our society that many don't even know of its existence, let alone question it. But what is it? In short, it is a political ethos whereby everything is viewed as a commodity – everything can be bought and sold.

Neoliberalism was introduced in the 1980s, during the Thatcher and Reagan years. It gives power to the top echelons of society – those in the richest 1 per cent. And that power not only keeps them rich, but also gives them more power the richer they get. Given via a public mandate, the power allows them to create governmental policies that aid and enable their goals further.

When I first learned about neoliberalism, I presumed it was something positive – a group of people coming together for a better, more equitable future. The name is confusing: liberalism immediately brings to mind freedom, 'new-age liberals', the hippies and those labelled so often as 'woke'. The word neo indicates that it is perhaps a new approach to liberalism and reminds me of the character Neo, played by Keanu Reeves in the film *The Matrix*. Neo's task was to wake up society from the suppression and control of the Matrix. So neoliberalism sounds as if it could be a movement for the better of humanity. Don't be duped by the name, however, because it is something far more sinister.

There are three main facets of neoliberalism:

- The privatisation of public services and organisations (such as healthcare, energy and education), transferring

ownership to the private sector to increase private
profits, accompanied by deregulating industries, so
that these private organisations and profits can grow,
unhampered by rules and restrictions.
- The reduction of tax (both personal income and
corporation), encouraging the growth of private wealth.
- A reduction in public spending, achieved via the
privatisation in the first facet (above), combined
with restricting welfare and benefits, capping
governmental costs.

Neoliberalism operates what is known as a 'free-market philosophy'. It is all about private profits, creating unrestricted private wealth by removing any of the state barriers and boundaries usually present in capitalism, which may prevent this.

The current era of harsh austerity measures allow the rich to become richer, with government only helping when the free-market economy or profits are at risk. An example here is the cost of energy bills in the UK. The UK energy industry was privatised in 1990, creating what is now often referred to as the 'Big Five' (originally big six) energy companies: British Gas, EDF, E.ON, OVO Energy and Scottish Power. At the time of writing, there are twenty-two energy companies operating in the UK, with several others having recently gone bust. With wholesale costs of gas and electric spiralling out of control in 2022 and 2023, the government responded with their 'energy bill support' scheme. Despite interviews and press briefings to the contrary, this scheme ultimately intended to keep the large energy companies in profit, rather than helping individual households. A £400 credit was therefore applied to each household's energy account, alongside the introduction of a price cap to the unit costs for energy. The UK government arranged to pay costs above the price cap to the energy companies and the £400 credit received by consumers also went direct to the fuel companies from governmental coffers. No actual money was seen by households. Many of these companies went on to report bumper profits, with Centrica, the parent company of British Gas, reporting their highest ever profit of £3.3 billion in 2022, up from £948 million in 2021. While the public struggled, the rich kept on getting richer. Neoliberalism at its finest.

With increased profits, the rich become more powerful, with little regulation of their activities, allowing them to accumulate ever more wealth and influence. The latter can be wielded over governments (often in the form of large donations and related 'advice'), exerting pressure for changes in policy that are even more favourable to them. All of this is achieved by turning the average citizen into a commodity: they become consumers of everything, from their healthcare to their education; everything is given a price, regardless of whether it should be under private control or operated for financial gain. Everything and everybody has a monetary value, with measurable metrics. So children become an investment, but not in a positive way – in a way that views them as the consumers and creators of more wealth for the ruling rich of tomorrow.

The linguistic theorist Professor Noam Chomsky is an outspoken critic of neoliberalism, stating:

> Neoliberal democracy? Instead of citizens, it produces consumers. Instead of communities, it produces shopping malls. The net result is an atomized society of disengaged individuals who feel demoralized and socially powerless. In sum, neoliberalism is the immediate and foremost enemy of genuine participatory democracy, not just in the United States but across the planet and will be for the foreseeable future.[1]

What happens to those disengaged individuals who grow up in a childist society? They allow the childism and the neoliberalism to continue unchallenged, from generation to generation. In fact, the more demoralised and disengaged they are, the better for those in power, because they are far easier to control.

How does neoliberalism influence childism?

Neoliberalism creates inequality in society, with children being the ones who are discriminated against the most. Children fall victim to poverty and the ever-increasing struggles of their families to keep a roof over their heads and food on the table. They fall victim to the emotional trauma and stress this poverty causes to parents, resulting in them using harsher parenting methods. They fall victim to the underfunding and privatisation of services.

Childism and neoliberalism snake through all elements of a child's life, impacting the most important services for children, the three that are most damaged being education, childcare and children's mental-health support.

Neoliberalism and education

Neoliberalism-ruled education means a huge focus on numbers, targets, rankings, exam results and league tables. Education becomes just another product and, as with all other huge industries creating products today, the powers that be hold those who work in it to account, measuring performance and assessing whether they are worthy of their investment.

Increasingly, there is a move towards turning schools into corporations, with the last decade seeing the introduction of multi-academy trusts (MATs) in the UK, run by managers and CEOs, rather than headteachers. Speaking about the government's plan to encourage more schools to join MATs in the future, the education secretary at the time, Gavin Williamson, said: 'The difference with the multi-academy trust model, and we see it again and again, is that the strongest leaders can take responsibility for supporting more schools, developing great teachers and allowing schools to focus on what really matters – teaching, learning and a curriculum that is based on what works.'[2] Despite this governmental push, however, research into the effectiveness of MATs is inconclusive.[3]

Neoliberalist education means children become the measurable data, as well as products of the system. They are viewed as an investment because they are the future employees of tomorrow, and these future employees will produce more profit for the organisations they end up working for, as well as paying income tax and becoming consumers, generating even more profit for the companies they buy from. Have you ever wondered why careers events at schools so rarely encourage self-employment as a valid career option?

Our schools today are all about conformity. From the age of four, children already have a life path mapped out: at sixteen, they will either leave education and start a government-approved apprenticeship or stay on at school or college, until eighteen, when they will either leave and start work (for somebody else) or go to university (for which they will most likely accrue an enormous debt) and then get a job. All routes lead to children being educated in such a way that they become good employees, feeding more money into the machine, not questioning the system.

Neoliberalism's obsession with creating 'work-ready' individuals, whether at the age of eighteen or twenty-one, means that there is little space (or funding) for subjects and lessons such as the arts, which help to fuel individuality or creativity. Schools are potentially problematic for neoliberalism – because if children are taught to think critically, rather than becoming passive, good employees, they could rise up and fight to end it as adults. It is in the neoliberal government's interest to prevent this from happening – children are seen as consumers of the future and the government would not be making a good investment if its money was spent on bringing about its own downfall. On this topic, Margaret Sims, honorary professor at the University of Macquarie in Sydney, Australia, says:

> [Neoliberalism has had] a devastating impact on the early childhood sector with its focus on standardisation, push-down curriculum and its positioning of children as investments for future economic productivity ... Unfortunately this focus on employability and future careers means that focus on certain subjects and curriculum is reaching down to younger and younger children, who should be playing and exploring nature, but are instead having times tables drilled into them.[4]

So often, neoliberalist education is reduced to teaching children to pass exams, rather than embracing their innate drive to learn and truly educating them about the world.

If neoliberalism means that schools are in danger of becoming mere exam factories, it follows that school discipline is becoming increasingly harsh. If children are not getting their holistic educational needs met, it is harder for them to thrive at school, and many will struggle with their behaviour in a system that is designed with numbers, not children, at its heart. Special educational needs and disabilities (SEND) support is consistently underfunded in neoliberalist education, with long waiting lists for diagnoses (three years or more is not uncommon). And even with a diagnosis and an Education, Health and Care Plan (EHCP) in place at school, many children with SEND still do not receive the support they need. Often, they are on the end of increasingly harsh punishments at school because there are not enough staff members to support them, and they are expected to fit in like a square peg in a round hole. A disproportionate number of children with SEND are excluded from school, with estimates that at least a third of children with ADHD have been excluded from school temporarily, and around one in ten has been permanently excluded at some point from the school system.[5] These childist, indeed ableist (discriminating against children with disabilities), policies send out a clear message: that there is no place for children in the system if they do not embrace and fit within it.

With pressure from governmental departments, OFSTED and an obsession with standardised testing and attendance figures, it is no surprise that so many schools are resorting to zero-tolerance policies. The real problem, however, isn't children's behaviour, but the system that has been designed for them. Neoliberalist education is fixated on numbers, results and measurable performances, valuing these over the wellbeing of children and their teachers.

At this point, I would like to ask you two questions:

1. Article 23 of the United Nations Convention on the Rights of the child, which covers the rights of children with disabilities, including SEND, states: 'Parties recognize that a mentally or physically disabled child should enjoy a full and decent life, in conditions which ensure dignity, promote self-reliance and facilitate the child's active participation in the community'. With this in mind, do you believe the current SEND provision in schools and the exclusion rates for children with ADHD are childist?

2. Article 29 of the United Nations Convention on the Rights of the child states, 'Parties agree that the education of the child shall be directed to the development of the child's personality, talents and mental and physical abilities to their fullest potential'. Do you believe that the current neoliberalist education system fosters or hinders this endeavour?

The impact of neoliberalism, sadly, doesn't end when children turn eighteen and enter the world of adulthood. Arguably, it cranks up a gear. In 1998, the government at the time introduced the idea of university tuition fees, something that had been abolished in 1976. The devolved governments in Scotland and Wales introduced their own fee structures.

University students are now seen as consumers, not learners. An act passed in 2004 meant that university students in England could be charged up to £3,000 per year of study; by 2010, this fee had trebled to £9,000 per year. Universities had become yet another victim of neoliberalism, moving from places of free thinking, free speech and free education to businesses clamouring to advertise and market their wares, in order to attract fee-paying customers. While you may be wondering why I have included information about university in this chapter, given that most children have turned eighteen by the time they attend (and indeed, are adults, not children), for those with a son or daughter at university, I can guarantee that they still view them as a child. The change to funding also indiscriminately impacts children, as university is the natural continuation of their childhood education for many.

How else do you ensure the highest returns for your money if you are running an education business? By keeping the salaries of your employees low and the demands on them high. Teachers and university lecturers are not paid enough. They are highly educated and skilled, having put themselves through a minimum of four years of higher education, graduating with an average debt of around £60,000 (which rises significantly each year, due to ridiculously high interest rates). Despite many members of the public thinking teachers have an easy life, they aren't actually paid for school holidays (instead, their salary is spread monthly, making it appear that they are being paid for the weeks they are off), and they start early and finish late, outside of school hours, frequently working into the evenings and weekends. Teacher pay has been frozen for years, meaning, in real terms, pay cuts when compared to inflation and the cost of living. Many university lecturers have historically been employed on zero-hours contracts, with no job stability, frozen pay and decimated pensions. Teaching staff are disillusioned, with major staff-retention and initial-recruitment issues. Because of this, 2023 saw many teachers and university lecturers strike over pay and working conditions. But who are the real losers in all of this? Once again, it is the children. They miss valuable education days and are affected by a lack of continuity due to a constant stream of cover teachers. University students have missed significant chunks of teaching time, potentially impacting their grades and therefore future prospects. At the time of writing, my own child is currently in the final year of his undergraduate degree, and strikes by university lecturers mean that he has had to sit exams and write assessments for modules, worth 50 per cent of his final-year grade, having had very few in-person lectures or seminars. To add insult to injury, a recent marking and assessment boycott by lecturers means that it is unlikely that these exams and assessments will be marked, with many students unable to graduate as a result. While I of course empathise with the impossible position of teaching staff, it is always the children that are most affected by our neoliberalist, childist education systems.

Neoliberalism and childcare

Parents today are faced with an impossible choice: do they focus on caring for their infant children, responding to their instincts to stay close to them and honouring their needs for attachment, or do they work every hour that God sends, in order to pay the bills? There is little support in society for parents who choose to stay at home to raise their children, and equally little for those who choose to return to work. The former are problematic in the eyes of the neoliberal because they are no longer working and paying into the system – as American author and politician Madeleine Kunin states: 'Every time a woman leaves the workforce because she can't find or afford childcare, or she can't work out a flexible arrangement with her boss, or she has no maternity leave, her family's income falls down a notch. Simultaneously, national productivity numbers decline.'[6]

The emotional and economic challenges of the early years could be made much easier if all families had access to good-quality, affordable childcare. Sadly, however, neoliberalism means that childcare is just another commodity, driven by profit, while parents are the pawns in the system, sometimes working to earn just enough to pay for childcare, with little left over for anything else. Then what of the children? They find themselves separated from their parents prematurely because parents cannot afford to take much time off after they are born and instead put them into childcare that is stretched to the limit because of inappropriate government funding. Once again, the children are the losers.

Since 2020, the UK childcare market has been estimated to be worth £6.7 billion, with the author of the report containing this estimation, business intelligence provider LaingBuisson commenting: 'Strong historic growth and a socially responsible profile continue to make this market attractive for investors looking for safe havens for their money.'[7] Childcare is increasingly privatised, the companies running daycare centres often attempting to turn care into a for-profit business, which is where the humanity of what they do suffers at the hands of neoliberalism. Care in all forms (whether for babies, the elderly or those with disabilities) is undervalued, the staff are underpaid, public funding is insufficient, working environments are inadequate and job security and satisfaction are low. Staff turnover is therefore high and it is those in care, or specifically, once again here, the children who suffer. The solution to the care crisis isn't to privatise it further because that means a focus on profits and not people. And the more childcare is privatised, the more expensive it will be for parents, who are already stretched to their limits.

While childcare can be a profitable business in the hands of large private companies, it is a different story for those who work in it and those who run small, independent settings. Childcare workers are some of the most underappreciated and underpaid in the workforce. Almost a fifth of those working in daycare centres and nurseries, aged twenty-three and over, earn less than the national living wage (NLW), with average childcare salaries ranging between £14,000 and £24,000 per year.[8] These low wages are not because childcare staff are unqualified – far from it, 80 per cent of staff are qualified to at least level three (the equivalent of A levels in the UK) and a third are qualified to level six (degree level).[9] Given the level of training and the demands of the job, why are childcare workers so underpaid? Is it because, in a childist and misogynistic society, we do not value the physical and psychological care of children as a valid career choice? Is it because the work of raising children that has historically been done by women, by mothers, for generations has always been undervalued, unseen and unrewarded? Arguably, raising the next generation should be one of the most important and highly paid jobs, but the reality is far different, thanks again to neoliberalism. On this idea, Professor Peter Moss, based at the UCL Institute of Education, says:

> It seems to us that a crisis is occurring – or rather crises. Now is the time for those of us in early childhood who find the influence of neo-liberalism deeply problematic and unpalatable 'to develop alternatives to existing policies', grounding them in ideas that contest neo-liberalism. We need to reimagine early childhood education and care as a public good, a collective endeavour and a right of citizenship.[10]

The cost of childcare varies greatly around the world. In the UK, the average cost of a full-time nursery place outside of London, is around £1,000 per month, with full-time places costing up to almost £15,000 per year in some cases. In Germany, where childcare has been subsidised by the state since 2013, the cost is on average around 50 to 150 euros per month, depending on location, family situation and hours needed.[11] A couple with dual incomes on an average salary in Germany will pay around 1 per cent of their income on childcare, compared to the UK where they will spend around 30 per cent of their salary, and the USA, where 23 per cent of a joint average salary will be used for daycare.[12] For those who are parenting on their own, these costs often mean that they are unable to work, however much they want to, because there is simply not enough income to live on after childcare costs are paid.

In March 2023, the UK government announced a huge expansion of funded childcare, a plan they claimed would take two years to come to fruition. The plan includes first offering fifteen funded hours per week (for thirty weeks of the year) to those with eligible two-year-olds, with phase two seeing the age of eligibility reduced to nine months (and up). The final phase of the plan which, at the time of writing, is set to happen by September 2025, would see thirty hours per week of funded care (for thirty weeks per year) for babies and children aged from nine months and above. While initially appearing to be a positive and welcome initiative for working families, the finer details indicate that the plans are perhaps more an attempt at a hollow vote grab before the next general election. The announcement has been met with grave concern from those who work in the childcare industry, as – predictably – the scheme is grossly underfunded. Where nurseries realistically need to receive funding in excess of £8 per hour to meet their costs, government funding is likely to be less than £5 per hour. Currently, nurseries make up the £3 per hour (or thereabouts) shortfall through charges to parents of babies and younger toddlers; however, this will no longer be possible with the new government plans, the result being significantly more financial strain on the already overstretched early-years sector, with a looming staff recruitment-and-retention crisis (nobody knows where the extra desperately needed early-years staff will come from to meet the inevitable new demands) and potentially the loss of several settings which will struggle to stay open because of the financial pressure that comes with providing more so-called 'free' childcare. Parents already struggle to find nursery spaces for their babies and toddlers; sadly, things are going to get much worse over the coming years if the government proceed with their plans.

Perhaps the most important consequence of the new announcements, given the focus of this book, is that the government have decided to change the carer/child ratio from 1:4 to 1:5. This means that children will have less direct supervision, less one-to-one time and less connection with their keyworkers, as already thinly spread childcare workers are stretched even more. This change in carer/child ratio is in direct conflict with a child's need for attachment, and despite many in the early-years sector having voiced concerns prior to the announcement, neoliberalist politicians decided to ignore them and forge ahead with their plans, regardless of whether they are good for children or not.

The new government childcare proposals also predictably overlook parents who choose to stay at home with their children. Once again, this is a childist viewpoint and one that also raises feminist concerns, since the majority of stay-at-home parents tend to be mothers. If funding (albeit incredibly scant) is being made available for children to be cared for by others outside of their homes, why can it not be made available for them to be cared for by their parents in their own homes? Arguably, this is an investment that would likely pay dividends in the future, enabling close attachments and connections for the children and improving the economic status of families who are struggling and living below, or close to, the poverty line while caring for their children themselves. One sensible argument here is for funding to be assigned to the individual child, allowing their parents or carers to choose how to spend it. Some may choose to take care of their children at home, using the funding to help the family's finances, while others may choose to put it towards a childminder, nanny or nursery. In this instance, the nurseries would be free to set a fee, with parents topping up any excess after the funding had been applied. This would leave the nurseries in a significantly better situation than they will be with the existing plans. And, ultimately, what is good for the nurseries is likely to be better for the children, too.

Alas, neoliberalism considers stay-at-home parents as 'economically inactive' and the new childcare plans are intended to get as many parents working, as quickly as possible after their babies arrive with as little governmental funding as possible. Profits over people and cash over care win out once again, with children suffering the repercussions.

Change is desperately needed in the funding and provision of childcare, but as long as politicians who do not value children, or their care, are in power and neoliberalism sees childcare as a commodity, it is likely that any changes made will be more detrimental than helpful to children, their parents and overstretched childcare workers.

Neoliberalism and children's mental-health support

Introduced by the charity Place2Be and launched in 2015, Children's Mental Health Week, which takes place in early February each year, aims to 'encourage more people than ever to get involved, spread the word, and raise vital funds for children's mental health'.[13] So here we are, back at the awareness mentioned by the Princess of Wales at the beginning of this chapter. But do we really need more awareness of children's struggles with their mental health?

It seems almost every other parent I speak to has or knows a child who is struggling. Thankfully, as a society, we are increasingly open to talking about mental health and our children are leading the way in being allies and spokespeople. There is always more awareness work to be done; however, it doesn't matter how much awareness there is if the funds are not there for appropriate support services. It is telling that the last aim of Children's Mental Health Week, as quoted above, is 'to raise vital funds for children's mental health'.

According to statistics, one in six children between the ages of six and sixteen has a mental-health condition.[14] Of particular concern are teenagers, particularly girls, with one in four struggling with their mental health. Waiting times in the UK for specialist mental-health support, known as the Child and Adolescent Mental Health Service (or CAMHS) are extremely long, with a recent freedom-of-information request submitted by the *Independent* newspaper showing huge variations in waiting times, depending on location.[15] Although in some areas children were seen promptly after referral, the average waiting time for an initial appointment was over three months, with some facing waits of up to three years. If a child is in crisis, every day counts, and three months is simply too long. Understandably, faced with the extremely long waits for state-funded help, many parents and carers seek help from charities, but most of these are overwhelmed and underfunded. It is common to be told that a charity cannot help unless the child is an active suicide risk (by active, most mean they have actually tried to kill themselves at least once recently). This is by no means the fault of the charities; again, it is because neoliberalism sees little profit in supporting mental health once as much of the care system as possible has been privatised. As a result, many families are left with the difficult choice between trying to privately fund therapy for their children or putting food on the table.

The closure of Sure Start centres

A quick mention must be given here to the underfunding of the Sure Start centre programme in the UK – a decision rooted in childism and neoliberalism.

Sure Start was launched in 1998 by then chancellor of the exchequer, Gordon Brown and minister for public health, Tessa Jowell. The scheme's aim was 'giving children the best possible start in life', which it aimed to do through community support and outreach services, improving early-years support for families. Sure Start Children's Centres were quickly opened in the late nineties and early noughties, with over 3,600 centres at the peak of the programme in 2009. They were focused in areas with the highest levels of deprivation, with a budget of over £500 million pounds allocated.

Sure Start centres offered much-needed support, advice and help for families, including parenting classes, baby and toddler groups, breastfeeding, weaning and healthy-eating help, antenatal and postnatal support, social support for parents, speech therapy and similar services, plus help for parents wishing to return to work. They soon became an important hub for those with young families and were well regarded throughout the UK. Research found that Sure Start centres were effective in their goals of improving the lives of children and their families, estimating that the service prevented 13,000 hospital admissions per year.[16] Children growing up in a Sure Start area were found to have a lower risk of being obese than those growing up in areas not served by a centre, and mothers who lived in a Sure Start area were found to provide a calmer, but more cognitively stimulating home environment and also used less harsh discipline methods.[17]

In 2005, the funding model of Sure Start was changed, moving more responsibility towards local authorities. This, along with further budget cuts imposed by the new coalition government in 2010 and a lack of appropriate funding by two successive Conservative governments has seen the loss of over 1,300 Sure Start centres, effectively closing almost one in three.

In February 2023, the government announced plans to fund new 'family hubs' in seventy-five areas of the UK, with a news release on their website stating, 'This announcement builds on the prime minister's ambition to put strong families at the heart of communities, in recognition of how important they are for people's life chances'.[18] It is ironic that this aim sounds remarkably like the goal of Sure Start, the service that has suffered so much through austerity measures. What has prompted the government to act now, after years of underfunding children's services and family support, remains to be seen, although it is likely neoliberalism is at play somewhere, just as it was when so many Sure Start centres were closed.

How austerity affects children

Austerity measures are becoming an increasingly popular neo-liberalist way for governments to reduce public spending, while working to promote the free-market economy. While the general public have to tighten their belts and count every penny they spend, there is myth that 'we're all in it together' and an attempt to muster a sort of Blitz spirit. But don't be deceived – austerity is most definitely not something that affects us all equally. It is a perfect opportunity for the rich to become richer and more powerful, while poorer families – especially the children – suffer.

At the time of writing, in the UK, approximately 4 million children are living in poverty, that's one in three of the 12 million British children. According to the charity Action for Children, 'A child is considered to be growing up in poverty if they live in a household whose income is below 60 per cent of the average (median) income for that year'.[19] In the USA, a recent census found that 16.9 per cent of children were living in poverty.[20] In England, the charity Shelter say that over 120,000 children are currently homeless and living in temporary accommodation, while the Trussell Trust say that demand for their food-bank services has increased by 81 per cent since 2018.[21] Between April 2021 and March 2022, the Trussell Trust distributed over 2.1 million emergency food parcels in the UK, with over 832,000 of them going to households with children. What sort of a society do we live in that food-bank usage is now normalised as a way of life, with politicians and even royalty popping up at their local food banks for PR and photo opportunities.

I have been volunteering for the charity Citizens Advice since early 2019, since which time demand for its services has increased exponentially. On the one day a week that I volunteer in the office I will speak to members of at least five families who are struggling with austerity measures, rising costs of living and inadequate support from the government. I speak to parents who are in tears, unable to provide their children with simple basics such as food, clothing and warmth, and who frequently go without meals so that their children can eat. In contrast to what you might read in the newspapers, these families aren't lazy scroungers; most people who claim Universal Credit are in work, but nobody has complete control over what life throws at them – illness, disability, redundancy, separation, divorce and bereavement don't usually feature in our life plans, and yet they can happen to the best of us. We are all one unexpected catastrophe away from living in poverty.

What happens to parents who are faced with this level of stress on a daily basis? One thing we do know, is that the more stressed parents are because of socioeconomic pressures, the more likely they are, according to research, to use harsher discipline methods.[22] Once again, the biggest victims of neoliberalism are children.

How neoliberalism impacts parents

As well as the economic pressures on parents caused by neoliberalism, the psychological pressure is immense. Parents are made to feel that parenting is something they must be brilliant at, and they feel guilty if they make mistakes. This applies even more so to mothers who decide to stay at home (SAHM) and raise their children full time. They are made to feel that they are contributing to neither the wider societal economy nor their family's budget. When mothers feel a failure economically, they can place more pressure on themselves to be 'a perfect mother', and when they inevitably fail at this, because no parent is perfect, this can leave them feeling even more worthless.

Neoliberalism not only causes but also thrives on parental problems – because the need to fix normal infant behaviour opens up yet another avenue for financial profit. The infant sleep industry, for example, is worth billions of pounds, with everything from sleep-training consultants and overnight nannies to mechanical replacements for human touch and expensive smart cribs that simulate rocking in arms. If parents weren't so exhausted, there would be no need for these products and services; but it is not in neoliberalism's interests to normalise infant sleep or other childhood behaviours that can be commercially monopolised.

Neoliberalism means that parents are more likely to pathologise normal child behaviour (for instance infant sleep) because the neoliberalist environment makes it almost impossible to work all hours to pay the bills *and* balance the normal nocturnal needs of a baby or toddler. Because it is so hard to function when they are burning the candle at both ends through parenting and full-time work, exhausted parents search for ways to 'fix' their child's behaviour, which they believe to be problematic (their sleep, say, which was never broken), rather than consider that the real problem is society and the impossible situation it has created for young families. Once again, the winners are neither parents nor children, but the owners of the companies who profit from parental desperation caused by the unsupportive society we live in.

Is there a future for anti-childism in politics?

For politicians to be actively anti-childist, they must care about children and their futures long after they have resigned and their party is no longer in power. Unfortunately, this is not how politicians work – their focus is on quick fixes, sound bites and statistics they can quote to convince the public to vote for them. True social change takes an investment in time as well as money. Programmes such as Sure Start were so forward thinking because they worked against the usual governmental goal of short-term results.

Neoliberalism suits politicians. With its focus on profit, not people, it produces metrics that can be spun to sway public opinion. This spin is often paired with governing through fear, be that fear of future economic disaster, fear of breaching rules, fear of fines, fear of losing liberties and even fear of global pandemics, environmental disaster and war. When a population is scared, it is far easier to control. As with authoritarian parents, influenced by the historical childcare experts, who seek to discipline through 'fear-of-God' measures, fear helps to keep governments in power and sneak neoliberalism into all aspects of life, while the public are preoccupied with worry.

There are so many other political issues that affect children through inherent childism that we have not even touched on in this chapter. Covid lockdowns and the fact that children, arguably, suffered the most when schools, nurseries, parks, groups and clubs were closed, when they were least affected by the illness itself. Brexit, when many of those in older generations voted for the future of children without truly considering the long-term effects for them. These are just two further examples, but the list is long and could fill a whole book. What we have covered here just scratches the surface of the issue, but I hope it's enough to open your eyes.

How do we change things? To start with, there needs to be more awareness of neoliberalism, its aims and its effects on our children. Only then will parents and child advocates be able to stand up to their childist governments and vote to create a more equitable future.

Rather than seeing young families as a drain on public funds, we should – rightly – see them as our future and invest in children, their parents and their carers appropriately. Children are the key to social and political change; we need to support and educate them in order that they can bring in a new breed of politics with a focus on connection and humanity, rather than the pursuit of profit over people. To do this, we have to recognise and call out childism when we see it. And we have to become actively anti-childist ourselves, something we'll cover much more in Chapter 8.

For now, let's move on to the last specific aspect of childism we will cover in this book: the question of a child's right to privacy and how our world violates it.

Chapter 6

Growing Up Online and
Violations of Privacy

*Children, I feel, are as much entitled to privacy
as human beings.*

BARBARA MERTZ, author

There is a meme, regularly shared on social media by those aged over forty. It says 'I'm so glad I grew up before cell phones existed. I did so many stupid things and there's no record of it anywhere.' This meme always pulls in a plethora of misty-eyed, nostalgic comments recalling good times, drunken nights, crazy events and foolish actions that would have resulted in a great deal of shame and embarrassment had they been caught on camera and shared online. I'm sure we can all remember events from our childhoods that we are glad weren't captured for posterity, shares and likes. Embarrassment, 'back in the day' before mobile phones existed, was limited to the collection desk of the local chemist, when we went to collect our processed 35mm films and quickly leafed through the blurry photos, red-faced and laughing with our friends. The most cringeworthy photos were quickly consigned to the dustbin, while others were either Blu-tacked to our walls for a couple of years, before being permanently discarded or left to fade in photo albums we only opened once a decade.

Growing up in an era where mistakes could be forgotten and our most embarrassing events remained private is a luxury that children today do not have.

The current generation of children live every aspect of their lives publicly. Everything is recorded and shared. Children have significant online footprints well before they reach adulthood, most created by their parents without their knowledge. The question that begs to be asked is: are child rights human rights if their information and images are being shared without their consent? Article 8 of the European Convention on Human Rights states: 'Everyone has the right to respect for his private and family life, his home and his correspondence'. And article 16 of the United Nations Convention on the Rights of the Child states: 'No child shall be subjected to arbitrary or unlawful interference with his or her privacy, family, home or correspondence, nor to unlawful attacks on his or her honour and reputation'. Despite this, children are regularly subjected to breaches of privacy, the effects of which can have lasting consequences.

Our society routinely shames children for entertainment. A few years ago, I came across a series of images on Facebook of children crying, looking terrified, confused, frustrated and angry, accompanied by light-hearted text, saying things like: 'My child cried because he got the blue cup, not the red one'; 'She was angry because I wouldn't let her wear her wellies to bed'; 'My son had a meltdown because I cut his sandwiches into squares, not triangles'; 'My daughter had a tantrum because I wouldn't let her eat Play-Doh'; and, 'He was terrified when his dad shaved off his beard and he didn't recognise him!' Others were invited to submit photos of their own children in similar states. Thousands of comments were added with similar stories of dysregulated toddlers and preschoolers. Last time I checked, the post had been shared almost a million times. Can you imagine the social uproar if, instead of ridiculing children, that post had been about elderly residents in a nursing home? The photographer would have been quickly disciplined and most likely shunned within the industry. Those who had shared the post would have been shamed into deleting it quickly. Newspapers and TV channels would have reported on the shocking story, citing maltreatment and abuse of the privacy of the elderly adults concerned. When photos and posts feature children, however, it is a different story. They are fair game. They don't have a voice, and it's socially OK to share their most dysregulated moments for public entertainment.

Speaking of questionable social media posts featuring children, have you ever come across ones focusing on discipline, lauding the actions of parents, saying things like, 'This is what a good parent does! This is proper discipline!'? Two such posts stick in my mind.

The first was of two siblings who had been bickering, as all siblings do. Having grown increasingly frustrated, their mother had bought a supersized adult T-shirt and, using a Sharpie, had scrawled the words 'get along shirt' across the front of the T-shirt in thick black strokes. The children were then made to wear the T-shirt together, with both their heads through the shared head hole, stuck to each other's sides until they supposedly worked through their differences. The mother took photos of the children in the shirt and shared her creation with pride on social media. The children looked deeply upset and embarrassed. The post quickly went viral, attracting thousands of positive comments, like, 'Yes, Mama, that's how it's done, that's how you do proper discipline!' Now, a quick image search for the term 'get along shirt' reveals hundreds of copycat photos, some used as a form of discipline, others for cosplay. Some entrepreneurial crafters have even created their own get along shirts to sell on Etsy.

The second memorable post was from a dad in Ohio, USA, who, in 2018, decided to teach his ten-year-old daughter a lesson about bullying. The girl had been caught bullying another child on the school bus and was temporarily suspended from the bus service as a result. Her father responded by making her walk the 5-mile journey to and from school, in freezing weather, over three days. For some reason, he also decided to video his distressed daughter from the comfort and warmth of his car during the long commute and shared it publicly on Facebook, where it was viewed hundreds of thousands of times. The story was picked up by several news organisations and published on their websites with the girl's full name, meaning that for years to come she will be identifiable. Once again, the parent was lauded for his good parenting skills, with few comments calling out the invasion of his daughter's privacy or the overly harsh discipline, and he himself reportedly said he didn't feel he had gone overboard at all.

Each December brings a new round of photos of distressed and uncomfortable children for our adult entertainment when Santa visits occur. Sobbing toddlers and preschoolers are forced onto Santa's knees and distressed babies are foisted into his arms, while they reach out for their parents, terrified by the separation and the big, jolly stranger in the red suit. These photos are considered a rite of passage. They are framed, copies are given to proud grandparents and they are shared on social media, where they are quickly met with heart and laughing emojis. It is rare that we stop to see the distress in the children's eyes or consider whether sharing these moments of intense discomfort is problematic. Indeed, anybody who comments to this effect is quickly met with accusations of being a killjoy or Scrooge.

Public sharing and shaming of children has become so ingrained in our society that most cannot see the problem with it. Yet, if similar images were shared featuring adults, particularly vulnerable ones, we would quickly rush in to protect their dignity and right to privacy. Why don't we do the same for children?

The future consequences
of growing up online

When we share cute pictures of our children online with friends and family, we rarely think about the impact of our actions ten or twenty years down the line. However, that cute picture of your baby son bathing in your kitchen sink or the sweet photo of your toddler daughter running around your garden half naked can have far-reaching consequences. Later in this chapter we will also talk about what happens when these images get into the wrong hands, and the safeguarding concerns involved in sharing our children's lives online, but for now, I want to focus on how they will feel about their lack of privacy in childhood when they grow up.

Several years ago, when one of my sons was in secondary school, his class were studying Internet security. (Note that, given the subject of this book, I do have my son's permission to share the following story.) The teacher asked all the children, then aged around fourteen, to put their names into an Internet search. My son searched his (fairly unusual) name and was horrified to find a photo of himself as a preschooler, wearing a princess dress. A decade previously, I had snapped a photo of him during a sweet game of dress up and, being proud of the absence of any gender stereotyping in our home, I had entered him into an online 'cutest princess' contest. Sadly, he didn't win, and I thought no more of the image. Until, that is, he came home from school after finding it online and told me how embarrassed he had been when his classmates teased him. I'd had no idea that the photo had been uploaded to the contest sponsor's website, where it had remained for years, alongside his name (although it was probably there in the small print had I paid enough attention to it). My son pleaded with me to get the image removed, and a couple of stern emails from myself later, the photo was taken down, along with his name.

This event caused me to seriously rethink the way I shared details of my children online. Although I had by no means been an oversharer, I vowed that I would never publicly share my children online again. I use social media sparingly for personal reasons, sharing only with a small group of friends, family and colleagues I know in real life, but even then, I am wary of what I share, including photos, videos and personal news, such as exam results. If I wouldn't be happy with my children sharing the same information about me publicly, then why should I have the right to share it about them?

We have no idea how information shared about our children online today will impact them as they grow older. What if they are applying for a job and part of the recruitment and vetting process involves searching their name online. What would they find? What might future romantic partners come across? Similarly, parents unknowingly create digital identities for their children online that can be permanent, the issue here being that these may not match the ones that they later choose for themselves. What will our children discover if they look back over our posts and social shares in a decade or two?

Research conducted by Microsoft found that 42 per cent of the teenagers aged between thirteen and seventeen who were surveyed said that they were unhappy with the information their parents had shared about them online.[1] Eleven per cent said that they felt their parents' oversharing was 'a big problem'. Research from the University of Michigan, USA, questioned children between the ages of ten and seventeen, and their parents, to find out what the children felt was OK, and what was not OK, for their parents to share about them online.[2] On the OK-to-share list was: positive content about participation in sports or activities and information that shows family life in a positive and happy way. Children agreed that parents should not share anything embarrassing, including naked baby photos, unflattering pictures or posts showing the children in a negative light (for example, relating to discipline and behaviour). The children also stated that they did not want anything shared that they felt should be kept private, such as images of them in bathing suits or information about who they may be dating. Unsurprisingly, there was a significant difference in opinion when it came to the question of asking for permission to share photos and information about children online. Children were more likely to believe that they should get a say in what was shared about them online than parents. Sarita Schoenebeck, Assistant Professor at the University of Michigan's School of Information commented on the findings[3]:

> It's easy to forget that the family and the home are considered private spaces in the US and that family members need to respect one another's privacy ... While teenagers can do things that are charming, funny, frustrating and sometimes enraging, parents should be thoughtful about whether that is appropriate content for sharing on social media.

A recent study conducted by a team of researchers from different universities in the USA found that many parents struggle to differentiate between sharing everyday information about their own lives and activities and those of their children and do not necessarily think about asking their children for their consent to post content related to them.[4] Interestingly, those parents who tend to share more content about their children online also tend to have children who engage in independent social media use at a younger age, posing a further potential risk to them. Other research has shown that over half of all parents regularly share sensitive personal information about their children online, such as date and place of birth, which may put the children at risk of security breaches and identity theft when they grow.[5]

The ethics surrounding parental sharing of their children

online are worrying. While most parents share with good intentions, love and pride, many are still doing so without the consent of their children, often embarrassing them, shaping a digital identity without consultation, and sometimes risking their children's livelihoods, relationships and safety in the future.

In 2016, an eighteen-year-old Austrian girl took her parents to court to force them to delete childhood photos of her that they had shared on Facebook without her consent.[6] The girl claimed that her parents had posted over 500 photos of her with 700 online friends and acquaintances and she felt that this oversharing was a violation of her privacy and human rights. The girl, who remained anonymous, spoke to a local newspaper about her case, saying, 'They knew no shame and no limits ... they didn't care if I was sitting on the toilet or lying naked in the cot. Every moment was photographed and made public.' The girl's father attempted to defend his position by saying that as her father and owner of the photos, he had a right to share them as he felt fit and did not need her consent.

In June 2018, Joseph Cannataci, the United Nations first Special Rapporteur on the Right to Privacy, warned parents that sharing their children's images on social media was a potential infraction of their human rights, stating that the rights of children needed to be upheld if their parents wanted to share their images. Cannataci referred to the 2016 Austrian court case, saying, 'We've already seen the very first cases of kids suing their parents because of the stuff they have posted on Facebook about them ... how do you deal with parents who insist on taking a video of their kids every single day and posting it on YouTube every single day?'

The Nirvana baby

In 1991, Spencer Elden, a four-month-old baby from California, USA, became one of the most famous infants in the world.

After lead singer of Nirvana, Kurt Cobain, watched a documentary on water birth and became obsessed with scenes of newborns 'swimming' underwater, Robert Fisher, then art director of Geffen Records (Nirvana's record label) decided to film a baby underwater for the cover of the band's second album, *Nevermind*. Fisher commissioned Kirk Weddle, a local specialist underwater photographer, to take some photos. Four babies were hired for the photo shoot, one of them being Spencer Elden, the son of a prop maker in the movie industry. Elden's parents were reportedly paid $250 for the hour-long photo shoot (the industry standard rate at the time). The image, in which Elden appeared completely naked, was later edited to include a dollar bill dangled on a fishhook in front of him, so that it looked like he was swimming towards the money. Nirvana's *Nevermind* went on to sell over 30 million copies, making it one of the bestselling albums ever. The cover image was also reproduced on posters which hung on the walls of millions of teenagers the world over. Elden's swimming-baby photo is arguably one of the most famous images of a baby.

Initially, Elden appeared to enjoy the fame and recreated the image a couple of times as a teenager and grown man (albeit with the addition of shorts), as well as popping up in the odd media interview when *Nevermind* celebrated a notable anniversary. In January 2022, however, then thirty-year-old Elden launched a lawsuit against Nirvana stating that the use of his image amounted to child pornography and that its usage had caused him permanent emotional distress. Elden stated that he believed Nirvana had intentionally used a pornographic image of him and that they had made millions of pounds from its use. He attempted to sue the members of Nirvana for $150,000 dollars each, including the estate of the late Kurt Cobain who died in 1994, only three years after the release of *Nevermind*. Originally, Robert Fisher, the art director, was named as a co-defendant, however this was dropped after he provided a statement which claimed that he had offered to edit Elden's exposed penis out of the chosen photo, but the band had preferred to keep the unedited, explicit version. The case was dismissed and Elden did not receive any compensation.

While Elden ultimately lost his case, the ethical ramifications for the wider issue of child consent are significant. It may have been almost impossible for Elden to prove that Nirvana knowingly distributed child pornography, but if the case instead focused on the lack of consent and breach of human rights – specifically the right to privacy – things may have been different. Whatever the outcome, this case certainly got the world talking about images of children and questioning who has the right to both share them and request that they are removed.

The ethics of selling products using children's images

The ethics of using images of children without their explicit consent to generate private profit is straight out of the neoliberalism playbook. Keen to share their little darlings with the world and make some money at the same time, parents sign their children up to modelling and talent agencies in the hope that they will become the next poster child for Lego or Johnson & Johnson or be the star of the next John Lewis Christmas advert.

Advertising has relied for decades on using cute children, especially babies, as a way to sell products. A prime example is Gerber, the American baby food and products brand, who have been using babies to sell their wares for almost a century. They now run an annual 'Gerber Baby' contest, which regularly sees entries from several hundred thousand families, all vying for their children to be the face of Gerber for a year (for which they are now paid $25,000). Three questions should be considered here:

1. Where does the money go? Is it kept in trust for the baby or do the parents spend it?
2. Can the baby give consent for their image to be used by such a huge company?
3. Are these contests and subsequent use of a baby's images and name in line with UN conventions concerning a child's rights to privacy?

Then there are the parent influencers on social media, who often make a very profitable living by sharing the ins and outs of their families' lives on social media. They can have huge followings, with those viewing their videos and photos invested in all aspects of their children's lives. They use these videos to sell everything from baby clothes and food to cars, holidays and expensive house remodelling. While many influencers have good intentions, and their accounts are often beloved by those who find their down-to-earth posts about daily family life reassuring, there is also a darker side. What will happen to the children who feature so heavily in their sponsored posts when they are grown? What impact does it have on their future privacy? Where does the money go? What will happen when the children are a little older and ask to not be featured in the sponsored posts? Or if, like the Austrian girl, they end up taking their parents to court to try to defend their right to privacy? If we use children as tools to make money online, we are walking a slippery ethical path along which we reduce them to the commodities of neoliberalism, making money from them when they are unable to fully understand the potential repercussions or give informed consent.

Some children may grow to love the fame they experienced, enjoying being spotted when out in public; others may find the attention far more difficult. Either way, when their images and videos are out there in the public domain, it is incredibly difficult to erase the identity that has been created for them. If we would not treat an adult in this way, as a profit-making tool, without their consent, why is it OK to violate the privacy of a child? If child rights are human rights, and all humans have the right to privacy, shouldn't this apply as a default setting, until the children are old enough to decide for themselves?

Data protection and children's rights

The General Data Protection Regulation (or GDPR) is an EU law adopted in 2016, centring on privacy and data protection. The regulation has an important role in the upholding of human rights, covering as it does all elements of data collection, handling, storage, processing and deletion for everyone – adult and child alike. However, children are afforded special treatment, with article 38 of the GDPR stating, 'Children require specific protection with regard to their personal data as they may be less aware of the risks, consequences and safeguards concerned and their rights in relation to the processing of personal data'.[7]

GDPR is primarily concerned with the processing of what is known as personal data. The following constitute personal data that may impact a child:

- Their full name
- Their date of birth
- Their place of birth
- Photos or video recordings of the child
- Their home address
- Their email address

GDPR states that personal data must only be collected, stored and utilised in a way that is strictly necessary. The regulation also gives privacy by design and by default. So, rather than parents and carers choosing to publish their child's personal information and presuming that it is OK to consent by proxy, GDPR starts from a position of affording the child privacy and assuming consent will not be given.

GDPR and the right to erasure

Another important part of GDPR, article 17 states that all individuals (whether adult or child) have the right to request that any personal data held or used by others be erased, even if they originally gave consent for it to be taken and used and even if that was done according to GDPR regulations. Basically, it affords individuals the opportunity to change their minds. This is commonly called 'the right to erasure' or 'the right to be forgotten' and can only be refused if there are specific and significantly compelling reasons to retain the information.

On children specifically, article 65 of the GDPR has the following to say about 'the right to erasure':

> ... is relevant in particular where the data subject has given his or her consent as a child and is not fully aware of the risks involved by the processing, and later wants to remove such personal data, especially on the Internet. The data subject should be able to exercise that right notwithstanding the fact that he or she is no longer a child.

This could prove a minefield in the future, with more and more court cases launched by those who felt they lacked privacy as children. The problem is that at this moment in time, few children and their parents are even aware of the existence of the GDPR.

What is the law on taking and sharing pictures of children?

Surprisingly, it is legal to take photos of other people's children in public places without permission from either parent or child. The law states that there is no reasonable expectation of privacy in public places, for either adults or children, and therefore there are no legal objections to taking photos or recording videos in a public place, whoever may be in them. If, however, a child is in a private place, such as their own home or garden, the law is different because there is then a reasonable expectation of privacy. Of course, the legality of taking photos of children in public places is different if the images are considered to be indecent.

Sharing photos of other people's children on social media also does not break any specific laws; however, it could be argued that it breaches article 8 of the European Convention on Human Rights and article 16 of the United Nations Convention on the Rights of the Child, both of which give individuals, including children, a right to privacy. These images could also break the GDPR, when they consist of personal data, in which case both the child and their guardians could request the images to be deleted, stating the right to erasure, as granted under the GDPR. If the individual or group responsible for posting the image refuses to delete it, most social media sites have specific reporting options for requesting the deletion of an image due to privacy violations.

If children are at school or nursery, parents should be asked for written permission to share their child's images online, on a website or social media channels and in school or nursery emails. This permission also applies to using images of children in printed materials, such as a hard-copy prospectus. Children should also be asked to give consent for the sharing of their images and other personal information, such as using their names in news reports or newsletters. Sadly, however, consent from children is rarely sought.

Child protection and safeguarding issues

The issues of consent and violation of privacy should be enough to put a stop to the sharing of children's personal information without permission (from both the parent or carer and the child). However, there are even more problematic reasons why we should be reluctant to share our children online – because often, the information shared can put them at risk:

- A child (and their parent or carer) who is hiding from an abuser may be at risk if they and their location are identified online.
- A child may be estranged from their family for a specific reason, and not want to share information about their life, including their location and activities.
- There is a risk of grooming when a child's personal information, such as the name of their school (with visible logos on uniform) or location, is shared, making it easier for groomers to target them.
- Those sharing images have no control over how they are used in the future. They can be downloaded and saved, screenshot and kept by others without the person who shared ever being aware. Even if an account is private, there is always a risk of it being hacked, or a risk posed by online 'friends', who they may not know as well as they think they do.

Many are aware of the existence of the dark web. What they are often not aware of, however, are the many disturbing areas of the dark web where innocent images of children are shared for criminal and perverted activity; for instance, they can be easily manipulated, using AI, into pornographic pictures, which are then sold on to paedophiles. Many paedophiles have specific fetishes, such as pictures of children in school uniform or in bathing suits, so that back-to-school images or ones of children enjoying themselves swimming on holiday can end up in paedophile rings, via the dark web. Basically, a photo or video of a child does not have to be explicit in any way for it to be of interest to paedophiles.

This may all sound far-fetched, but the statistics paint another picture. In 2021, German police investigated and managed to close down a dark-web platform known as Boystown.[8] Boystown was believed to be one of the largest child-porn dark-web platforms, with over 400,000 active members. As the name suggests, most of the photos and videos shared were of young boys, but images of girls also featured in the million posts made by members in the two years the platform was active. Many more similar platforms still exist, with photos and videos of children taken and shared innocently by loving parents and carers being manipulated and distributed among those subforums with special fetishes. Research has previously indicated that while paedophilia sites make up only 2 per cent of dark-net sites, 83 per cent of dark-net traffic is generated by those seeking to access the material; commenting on their findings to *Wired* magazine, lead researcher, Dr Gareth Owen, commented: 'Before we did this study, it was certainly my view that the dark net is a good thing. But it's hampering the rights of children and creating a place where paedophiles can act with impunity'.[9]

It seems the only way that parents can effectively protect the privacy rights of their children and ensure that their images will not end up on these sites is by not sharing them online in the first place.

Other invasions of child privacy

Given what we have just discussed, it is understandable that parents are growing increasingly anxious about their children's safety. This is a worry that has been pounced on by businesses, keen to make money from parental anxiety.

A quick Internet search for 'child tracking app' returns over 350,000 results, while 'child tracking device' returns over 425,000. Worried parents can purchase apps to download on their children's phones, so that they can monitor their every move, furthermore, tracking bands, smart watches, tags, keychains and various other child GPS tracking devices are also available. These can all make parents feel a little more relaxed, and also generate big profits for businesses, but what impact are they having on our children? Are these apps and devices inherently childist, prioritising adult feelings over the privacy rights of children?

Research looking into the legalities of a range of child mobile tracking apps found that over 70 per cent of them violated an American law aimed at protecting children's privacy online.[10] In addition to violating human privacy rights, the study authors registered concern that if the devices were hacked, they could give out sensitive information about children's locations and movement patterns, as well as their identities, which could put them at risk. Commenting on their findings, Dr Kanad Basu, Assistant Professor of Electrical and Computer Engineering, said, 'Suppose the app collects information showing that there is a child on Preston Road in Plano, Texas, downloading the app. A trafficker could potentially get the user's email ID and geographic location and try to kidnap the child. It's really, really scary.' Could it be that our very attempts to keep children safe are not only violating their rights to privacy but are also actually putting them at increased risk, too?

The growing use of child tracking apps and devices by parents also poses a question of trust. If parents trust the devices more than they trust their own children, what sort of a message does this give to children? If they grow up believing their parents do not trust them, this could cause huge rifts in connection and relationship difficulties, resulting in a loss of trust in their parents and feeling they are no longer able to confide in them about big issues.

There is also the possibility of increasing anxiety for children. Children today already have to contend with endless messages about the wrongs of the world and the risks that surround them. If they grow to believe that the world is inherently dangerous and that the only way to keep safe is to use trackers, then it is likely that we will see more anxiety and a damaging effect on confidence. A constant wariness of others can become yet another difficult issue for teenagers to tackle – teens who already have record levels of anxiety.

We also need to truly consider the concept of consent. Are children really consenting to carry these trackers? Do they truly understand the repercussions of an online app tracking their every move – the possibility of the data being hacked and the risks that brings? Are they even being asked for their consent at all? Like GDPR, should we give children privacy by default?

Finally, we come back to neoliberalism, where children and their safety are seen as a commodity that can be manipulated for maximum profit. When we download the apps and buy the so-called safety trackers, we are buying into the idea, yet again, that child rights can be breached if enough money and fear are on the table. It is in the interests of the companies manufacturing these products to make both children and their parents scared – because fear sells. As always with neoliberalism, children are the real victims, with the most to lose.

I'd like to end this chapter by asking three questions:

1. Article 8 of the European Convention on Human Rights states, 'Everyone has the right to respect for his private

and family life, his home and his correspondence'.
With this in mind, if child rights are human rights,
why is it socially acceptable to share photos of children
in distress when they are clearly identifiable, whether
through the use of their names, locations or even
just their appearance? Is it OK to shame adults for
entertainment and violate their privacy in this way?

2. Article 16 of the United Nations Convention on the
Rights of the Child states: 'No child shall be subjected
to arbitrary or unlawful interference with his or her
privacy, family, home or correspondence, nor to
unlawful attacks on his or her honour and reputation.'
Is the sharing of young children's personal information
for use in advertising and selling products on social
media in contravention of this code given that they are
too young to give fully informed consent or understand
the long-term consequences?

3. Is the tracking of children a violation of their rights
of privacy? Are there human-rights implications to
tracking them, especially when there is significant profit
to be made from the sale of tracking devices? Would we
consider it acceptable to track adults in the same way?

Time for change

In Chapters 1–6, we have looked at the various forms of childism
facing children today – from popular parenting methods, based
upon the outdated views of the historical childcare experts, to
state-sponsored childism and the violations of privacy that children are faced with on a daily basis.

I hope you have a clearer view now of what childism is, and
how it affects us all. Because we were young once and we have all
lived through much of the discrimination covered in the pages of

this book, this discrimination has shaped us, just as it will shape our children and those in generations to come, unless we stand together to call for change.

It is possible to live in a world without childism – a world that would look very different from the one we live in today. But what would it look like? That's exactly what we will discover in the next chapter.

Chapter 7

Imagine a World Without Childism

Every generation of children offers mankind the possibility of rebuilding his ruin of a world.
EGLANTYNE JEBB, British social reformer and founder of Save the Children

While educating adults about the importance of kindness, altruism, empathy and acceptance is important, the best chance we have of building a society that is free of discrimination and anti-social behaviour is by focusing on children. And by this, I don't mean giving them more lessons on hate crime or reading them more books about treating others with kindness; I mean treating them in the way that we hope they will grow to treat others. Actions speak louder than words.

It starts with parents, but the work that is needed to bring about an anti-childist movement in society needs the involvement of all adults, parents or not – those who teach children, those who take care of their health, those who look after them in their early years, those who entertain them, those who set laws and fight to uphold them and those who formulate and vote for policies that affect them. In short, every single one of us has a role to play (we will discuss this much more in the next chapter) and we can be the generation to start the shift and raise children who will change the course of society for ever. Both a scary and an exciting thought, isn't it?

What would a world without childism look like? It would certainly include the following:

- **Awareness of childism** The word 'childism' would be a part of everyday vocabulary; all adults (and children) would know what it means and be able to call out discrimination of children when and where they see it, without being met by ridicule and calls of being 'woke'. Adults would acknowledge the childism they faced in their own childhoods and how it has impacted them (there would be no more claims of 'it never did me any harm') and vow that their generation will be the last to experience it.

- **Being informed about child development** All adults who come into contact with children would be educated about their physical and psychological development. Expectations of children would be realistic and we would no longer attempt to train them to behave in ways that are too advanced for their age. This means there would be no sleep training or products aimed at prematurely separating infants from their primary carers. The system would honour and be designed around the holistic needs of children. The importance of the early years and the impact of the presence of involved parents during this period of development would be properly acknowledged, and childcare workers would rightfully be seen as the highly skilled and qualified workers they are, their significant societal impact being recognised.

- **Anti-childist forms of discipline** We would finally move away from the teachings of the historical childcare experts, leaving behind discipline (both at home and at school) that focuses on shaming, punishing, hurting, excluding and ignoring children as a way to try to control their behaviour. We would see difficult behaviour as communication and seek to work collaboratively with children to uncover the problems and needs underpinning it. We would help children to regulate their emotions and realise how important it is for adults to be able to properly regulate their own, too. This type of discipline would focus on truly teaching and guiding and would be healing for children and adults alike.

- **Proper investment in children and their families**
  People would vote for parties that focus on children and who will genuinely improve the world for them, moving from neoliberalism to a type of politics that values humanity over money. Politicians would invest in children, families and the organisations that support them. The education system would be properly funded, with teachers valued and paid appropriately. The same would be true of healthcare, particularly mental health and SEND provision. The reduction of poverty and the end of austerity would be a major goal, with the recognition that poverty disproportionately affects children. We would be able to trust our politicians and see a new generation of empathetic ones attempting to heal, rather than spin and profit for their own good.

I understand that this sounds ridiculously utopian, but we have to start somewhere. So, why not aim big? Anything we can achieve would be better than the world we live in today, and if we don't have a goal, how do we know what to aim for?

In the rest of this chapter, I'd like to focus a little more on the potential impact of five specific areas:

- The impact of anti-childist discipline
- Night-time parenting and the impact of anti-childist sleep support
- The impact of an anti-childist government
- The impact of anti-childist education
- The impact of anti-childist mental-health support

The impact of anti-childist discipline

As we learned in Chapters 3–5, most discipline used today is highly childist. Whether we are talking smacking and spanking, yelling and shaming, time out and naughty steps or excluding children from our attention when they are struggling to behave 'well', these approaches all originate from the discriminatory teachings of the historical childcare experts. The methods advised by these experts, and those who have followed in their footsteps, imparting their advice in modern-day parenting books, websites and television programmes, all fall into the category of authoritarian parenting.

Identified by the American psychologist Diana Baumrind in the 1960s, authoritarian parenting is categorised by high levels of adult control combined with low levels of parental warmth. It is strict, inflexible parenting that asks too much of children, with a focus on obedience more than anything else. At the opposite end of the spectrum, sits permissive parenting, where parents are warm, but have no control over their children. They try to be their children's friends and are scared to discipline or make them cry. Boundaries are non-existent and they expect too little of their children, resulting in few attempts to guide and teach them more appropriate behaviours. Permissive parenting is as dysregulated as authoritarian parenting and can be just as damaging. Because expectations of children raised by permissive parents are low, they are often not encouraged to reach their full potential, and because a big part of permissiveness is based on the avoidance of upsetting them (with parents frequently 'giving in' to appease them), children can grow to struggle with regulating their emotions. If they don't learn to deal with frustration, anger, disappointment and the like as children, then as teens and adults they are more likely to lack emotion-regulation and impulse-control skills.

The sweet spot in the middle, is where the authoritative parent sits. Authoritative parenting is high in warmth and high in control – only the control is age appropriate and designed to teach and guide children. There are boundaries and limits, and there is discipline, but these are implemented mindfully, with the child's best interests and learning at heart (even though it may not feel that way to the child at times). Authoritative parenting is nurturing and loving, with good communication and boundaries upheld with non-punitive discipline.

In 2015, I wrote the first edition of *The Gentle Parenting Book*. In Chapter 1, I define gentle parenting as being focused on empathy, understanding, respect and boundaries:

> ... a holistic philosophy that embraces the emotional as well as practical aspects of parenthood. In gentle parenting children matter, but so do adults too. Parenting should be a dance between the needs of children and parents, with practice this dance can lead to something quite beautiful, with tremendous growth for both. For too long parenting has been viewed as a battle. A battle for control between parent and child. Some parenting methods give all control to the parents, for fear of the little tyrants becoming unmanageable monsters as they grow. Other methods give children far too much control, with parents scared to discipline, when necessary, for fear of upsetting their delicate offspring. Gentle parenting is all about finding a balance of control, giving children just enough, at a time when they can handle it, with parents enforcing appropriate boundaries and limits. Gentle parenting is about being

ever mindful of the long-term effects of a parent's actions as well as the immediate needs of safety and expectations of society.

Gentle parenting is simply authoritative parenting, just brought a little more up to date. And gentle parenting is the key to anti-childist discipline. You won't find any research showing its efficacy, though – the terminology is too new and undefined scientifically; so, instead, we can look at studies of the impact of authoritative parenting methods, of which there are many and which unanimously agree that it is the healthiest way of raising children.

Another concept to consider when investigating the impact of discipline style is the definition provided by American psychologist Martin Hoffman. Hoffman's model of discipline categorises methods as falling into one of three distinct categories: induction, power assertion and love withdrawal.

- **Inductive discipline** This style of discipline involves parents using reasoning, with a focus on understanding the child's behaviour and helping them learn how to behave in more socially appropriate ways. This is not done punitively, but rather in a way that teaches and guides.
- **Power assertion** This occurs when parents capitalise on their power over children, using it to control them; it often involves shouting and scaring children, hitting them, punishing, threatening, shaming and otherwise dominating them.
- **Love withdrawal** This is when children are ignored, sent away from their parent, or the parent otherwise makes them aware of their anger, frustration and disappointment without showing this physically. This includes time outs, naughty steps and ignoring 'bad behaviour'.

Hoffman found that inductive discipline carried significant benefits, resulting in better behaviour and moral development than discipline using power assertion or love withdrawal. Hoffman's inductive discipline is the style predominantly practised in authoritative and gentle parenting and, indeed, is the most supportive and least childist type. Non-discriminatory discipline should centre on teaching children to understand themselves in order to behave better and to solve their own problems, not punishing them for having them.[1]

When we look into research on the efficacy of inductive discipline, it is incredibly convincing. Children raised using an inductive style of discipline are more likely than their peers raised using more childist forms of discipline to have:

- fewer behavioural problems, both as young children and adolescents[2]
- better emotion-regulation skills, both as children and as grown adults[3]
- more empathy and prosocial behaviour (behaviour that is to the benefit of others in society), again in childhood and adulthood[4]
- more mature critical-thinking skills[5]
- better moral values, lasting throughout life[6]
- less substance misuse as adolescents[7]
- better peer relationships in early childhood and adolescence[8]
- less chance of smoking and drinking in adolescence[9]
- lower levels of obesity as adults[10]
- less depression in adolescence and adulthood[11]
- less anxiety in adolescence and adulthood.[12]

The last six points are particularly interesting. How does childhood discipline style impact the likelihood of a teenager smoking, drinking or taking drugs? How does it impact an adult's weight years into the future? How does it affect mental health decades away? The answer is that a child who experiences inductive discipline, authoritative, gentle or non-childist parenting (or whatever name you prefer to give it) is raised using collaboration and communication, rather than coercion and control. Coercion and control teach children from a very early age that they cannot trust their parents, especially not with their biggest feelings, emotions, secrets and needs. In fact, they learn to keep their feelings to themselves in order to avoid the physical pain and fear of power assertion and the emotional pain of love withdrawal; they learn to internalise emotions, with no safe person or space to share them with, or to be able to ask for help. And these feelings don't just go away. They tend to grow and infringe more and more on the growing child's morale and mental health. Unable to free themselves of psychological pain, teenagers and young adults reflect it inwards ever more, with self-harming behaviours, including alcohol and drug abuse. These repressed feelings can eat away at a child's self-esteem and self-confidence, and they are more likely to suffer from anxiety and depression as they grow. Finally, in a quest to fill the hole left by the love withdrawal, they look for other things to make them feel good – comfort eating, casual sex with multiple partners, smoking, drugs and alcohol. At its core, addiction is often caused by the pain inflicted by authoritarian, disconnected, fear-based parenting methods. As psychologist Gabor Maté explains in his book *In the Realm of Hungry Ghosts: Close Encounters with Addiction*:

> Not all addictions are rooted in abuse or trauma, but I do believe they can all be traced to painful experience. A hurt is at the centre of all addictive behaviours. It is present in the gambler, the Internet addict, the compulsive shopper, and the workaholic. The wound may not be as deep and the ache not as excruciating, and it may even be entirely hidden—but it's there. As we'll see, the effects of early stress or adverse

experiences directly shape both the psychology and the neu-robiology of addiction in the brain.[13]

Another element to consider with parenting styles is that authoritative, gentle and inductive discipline require parents and carers to be self-regulated. These methods place a focus on the adults being good role models, believing that parents should try to remain calm in order to help dysregulated children to reach emotional homeostasis.

Perhaps one of the biggest issues created by childism and harsh discipline techniques is that if adults were not raised in a com-passionate way, learning to regulate their emotions from calm parents, it becomes virtually impossible for them to pass on a skill that they do not possess themselves.

This is why it is so important that we are aware of childism and the impact it had on us, because in order to be the generation to change how children are raised, we need to re-parent ourselves and learn how to self-regulate. This is no easy task (and we should show ourselves grace when we slip up – something we will talk about a lot more in the next chapter).

Can you imagine the impact if we raised a generation of chil-dren who were able to regulate their emotions well? This vision is one that spurs me on when I am struggling with my own self-regulation. Because I owe it to myself, my children and future generations of my family to try my best. But I also owe myself patience and empathy on the days when I am struggling – because as well as being part of the change, I recognise that I am also a victim of childism (we will come back to this in much more detail in the next chapter).

Night-time parenting and the impact of anti-childist sleep support

Historical childcare experts have adversely influenced night-time parenting for over a century, meaning parents avoid picking up their babies, scared of feeding or cuddling them too much in the mistaken belief that they will create bad habits and inhibit their child's ability to self-soothe. These messages are reinforced by an army of sleep trainers and coaches, an unregulated group who can net four-figure weekly salaries. Marketing of these services centres on making parents believe not only that their babies or toddlers have a sleep problem, but also that it is a problem so complex that they cannot fix it without expensive professional help. The help given by sleep trainers is not magic, though –in fact, it usually involves regurgitated historical childcare expert advice to encourage separation at the onset of sleep time, restricting feeding at night, implementing a solid bedtime routine and a lot of clock watching.

What would happen if instead we empowered parents to understand normal infant development? If they knew that baby and toddler sleep did not look like that of an adult and won't for several years. What impact would it have if adults were all aware of the importance of attachment and understood that 'clinging' and crying to maintain close proximity to their parents both day and night is the default state for infants, not a 'problem' that needs to be fixed? What if parents knew that night feeding was important throughout the whole of the first year of life? And that there is no such thing as self-soothing or creating bad habits? And what would happen if parents, once they were aware of the nuances of normal infant sleep, demanded more support and better adjustments for working parents with young families?

Sleep training and viewing child sleep as a pathological

problem that needs to be fixed is not only childist – it's also par-entist. It prevents parents from getting the support they need in order to meet the normal demands of raising a baby or young toddler. Every parent who shells out for expensive sleep-training advice, rather than lobbying their local MP to better meet the needs of young families is, ironically, making the problem worse.

Truly understanding the nocturnal needs and normal devel-opment of sleep in infancy, would allow parents to be more responsive to their children, which, unsurprisingly, is better for children. Research has shown that babies with more emotionally available mothers at night have lower cortisol levels than those with less emotionally available mothers.[14] Cortisol is a steroid hormone that is primarily responsible for the fight-or-flight stress response. While a little bit of cortisol is a good thing, higher levels are linked with increased stress – hence babies with less emo-tionally available mothers (for instance, those who are practising sleep-training methods such as controlled crying, pick up, put down, shushing and patting or disappearing chair) are exposed to more stress than those whose mothers are more responsive to their needs at night.

Similarly, co-sleeping (where the baby is in the parental bed or in a crib in the parents room) for the first six months also results in lower cortisol levels at age one, with higher maternal nurturance contributing to more optimal functioning of the HPA (hypothalamic-pituitary-adrenal) axis, controlling the body's response to stress.[15]

Further research looking into maternal nurturance during infancy has shown that babies who received more maternal support have more developed hippocampal regions of the brain at school age (the area of the brain linked to stress modulation). Less stress in infancy is linked with better emotion regulation as children grow and also has an impact on attachment between children and their caregivers.[16] Research has shown that toddlers who have strong attachments sleep better at night than their less-well-attached peers, therefore it is likely that nurturing, responsive childcare at night will ultimately make for calmer, better-attached children, which can only make life happier and easier for parents, too.[17]

The impact of an anti-childist government

Chapter 5 looked at what I term 'state-sponsored childism', the problem of neoliberalism and the effects of growing up (and raising a family) while living in poverty. What sort of an impact could an anti-childist government have if they funded children's services properly, and took real, tangible steps towards ending poverty and not just short-term promises to rally public opinion for the next election? Of course, this requires long-term thinking, with policies and programmes put in place today, the efficacy of which may not be proven for many years, likely long after the founding government have left office.

Research has shown that living in poverty for four years during childhood has a significant impact on how children behave among their peers, with those with the most difficult behaviour experiencing the highest levels of poverty.[18] A reduction in poverty would therefore likely see a reduction in antisocial behaviour for those children who would be lifted out of it. This would have a knock-on effect on how schools tackle classroom discipline (our next discussion point), taking pressure off them to some extent. We also know that growing up in poverty has a significant impact on adolescent mental health, so tackling it could also lighten the load of child mental-health services, and help to reduce the numbers of tweens, teens and young adults living with anxiety, depression and other mental-health issues today.[19] Research has also shown that government-backed financial interventions have a significant positive effect on reducing internalising symptoms (such as anxiety and depression) in adolescents.[20] A generation of happier, healthier children would have long-lasting impacts into adulthood, with far-reaching positive financial implications, including reducing demand for adult mental-health support and related benefits.

Reducing the number of children living in poverty and supporting families financially also has a positive impact on crime rates. Research in the USA, showed that enrolling families with low-income levels in a government-backed tax-credit scheme has a significant positive effect on reducing adolescent crime rates.[21] Further research in which mothers living in poverty were given unconditional cash payments throughout the first year of their children's lives, showed that the financial support had a big influence on the babies' developing brains, with areas associated with the development of cognitive skills most positively affected.[22]

Clearly, properly supporting families with young children when they most need help has far-reaching results, from reducing mental-health issues at all ages, difficult and antisocial behaviour and criminal activity to changing the way a child's brain develops. Of course, while these all have an enormously positive impact on the individual children and their families, solid investment in children and their families will also allow politicians to reap rewards in years to come as education, healthcare, policing and even the prison systems are all positively affected.

It seems a no-brainer to embrace measures reducing poverty. But alas, neoliberalism is designed to restrict the growth of the welfare state, the very opposite of what is needed to make politics genuinely anti-childist.

The impact of anti-childist education

Do you remember a time from your own childhood when you struggled at school? Maybe you found it hard to concentrate in class, you didn't revise for an exam, you failed to do your homework, you got into trouble for not paying attention or maybe you were rude to your teacher? How did the school deal with your behaviour? Were you given a detention? Removed from the class? Made to stay in at break time? Sent to visit the headteacher? Did those discipline efforts help to resolve the problems underlying your behaviour? Did they truly help to improve your education? Or did they leave you feeling disconnected from it? Can you imagine how your experience might have been improved if the approach had been anti-childist? If staff took time to understand what was going on for you and work out how they could help?

Of course, many people loved their time at school (I am one of them) – however, there are always things that could have made the time there more enjoyable and easier. What would they have been for you?

Anti-childist schooling would enable each child to find and follow their own passions. It would be creative as well as academic and it would nurture children as the whole and individual people they are. Perhaps your time at school could have been transformed if the education had been truly holistic and allowed you to thrive at the subjects you loved. What difference would that have made to your future education and life choices?

An anti-childist education system would understand the baggage that many children bring with them to school. It would be trauma informed and aware of the importance of attachment and relationships. Decisions would be more democratic, giving more of a voice to children. Importantly, the system would be appropriately funded, with happy, well-paid and appreciated teaching staff. There would be less of a focus on numbers, measurements and outcomes and more on meeting the needs of each individual child, so that they could be their best, whatever that looks like.

The late Sir Ken Robinson, author and education advisor, spoke widely of the importance of nurturing passions and encouraging creativity at school. His 2006 TED talk entitled 'Do schools kill creativity?' is mandatory viewing for anyone wanting to understand what anti-childist education looks like. Robinson spoke about the current aims of education with a narrow focus on academic achievement in a small number of specific subjects. He challenged this view and proposed that children need a new system, encouraging more creativity, rethinking what it means for a child to be 'successful'. In his book *The Element: How Finding Your Passion Changes Everything*, Robinson says:

> The fact is that given the challenges we face, education doesn't need to be reformed – it needs to be transformed. The key to this transformation is not to standardize education, but to personalize it, to build achievement on discovering the individual talents of each child, to put students in an environment where they want to learn and where they can naturally discover their true passions.[23]

According to Robinson, an anti-childist education system would be one where children would be able to develop organically, according to their own strengths and interests, rather than a neoliberalist one focused on churning out carbon-copy children, trained to bolster the economy by being good future workers. In his TED talk from 2006, Robinson said:

> We have to go from what is essentially an industrial model of education, a manufacturing model, which is based on linearity and conformity and batching people. We have to move to a model that is based more on principles of agriculture. We have to recognize that human flourishing is not a

mechanical process; it's an organic process. And you cannot predict the outcome of human development. All you can do, like a farmer, is create the conditions under which they will begin to flourish.

An anti-childist education is nurturing and sees children as individuals. It also values all subjects equally, allowing children to find their best fit in order to thrive.

In the mid-1990s, a group of educationalists and psychotherapists in the UK came together to work on designing a new anti-childist approach to education and behaviour management. 'Thrive' is described as a 'social and emotional development model that looked at children and young people's needs and provided responses and activities to engage them with life and learning'.[24] The four pillars underpinning Thrive are: 1. attachment theory; 2. child-development theory; 3. neuroscience; and 4. play, creativity and the arts. The Thrive approach uses these theories and underlying research to create training programmes for schools and early-years settings, with a focus on raising self-esteem and confidence in children, increasing their emotional wellbeing and improving communication, helping to encourage them to engage with their education. The training also helps teaching and early-years staff to understand the neurological causes of common tricky behaviours and to appreciate the differences in brain development occurring during childhood and how events, such as experiencing trauma, impacts this. This allows staff to form realistic expectations of a child's behaviour and helps them to understand how to support children better if they are struggling. Finally, the approach, and the new understanding it creates, helps teaching and early-years staff to feel calmer and more emotionally regulated themselves, enabling them to be better role models and encouraging co-regulation – where the feelings and emotions of both staff and children are taken into account, and safe spaces (both physical and metaphorical) are provided. Stress levels are then reduced and staff can be more attuned to the feelings of children when their own feelings are regulated. This brings about a feeling of mutual respect and improves connection, resulting in better behaviour, increased staff morale and healthier learning environments.

Positive relationships between teachers and students don't just improve problematic behaviour, they also improve relationships between students who struggle with their behaviour and their peers.[25] In short, everybody is happier when teaching and learning take place in a supportive, calm environment with a focus on co-regulation.

Punitive discipline policies, on the other hand, are not only stressful for children, but for teaching staff, too. The constant threats, yelling and punishing leave staff in a heightened state of stress, with children on high alert. When both children and staff are dysregulated, learning is inhibited and tricky behaviour is more likely to spiral out of control.

Anti-childist behaviour policies focus on improving children's social–emotional development and the teacher–student relationship, which research has found, coincidentally, to be the most effective approach to tackling behaviour.[26] Researchers have also found significant positive correlations between improving social–emotional learning skills, academic achievement and student happiness.[27] In short, zero-tolerance approaches make everyone, including staff, feel worse, as well as resulting in poorer behaviour and worse academic outcomes for children. Given this, it's surprising that these policies form the basis of most school's behaviour policies today, isn't it?

In 1994, in the USA, a multidisciplinary collaboration between educators, child rights activists and researchers who strongly believed that education should meet the social and emotional needs of children as well as their academic ones resulted in the birth of an approach known as CASEL (which stands for Collaborative for Academic, Social, and Emotional Learning).[28] CASEL is focused on five core competencies:

- **Self-awareness** The ability for individuals to recognise their own feelings, beliefs and values and how they impact behaviour.
- **Self-management** The ability to regulate our own emotions, controlling our impulses and working to reduce our stress levels.
- **Responsible decision-making** The ability to make decisions involving our own behaviour and interactions, based upon safety, ethics, social norms and the like.
- **Social awareness** The ability to empathise with others and to understand their points of view and differing beliefs, with a focus on respect.
- **Relationship skills** The ability to form healthy and meaningful relationships with others and groups, taking into account personal differences and beliefs.

These social and emotional learning (SEL) skills are arguably more important than academic ones and should therefore be a focus for teaching and childcare staff, both for the children in their care and themselves. Children who come from traumatic home environments, including those who live in poverty, are more likely to struggle with SEL skills, and therefore a holistic view that focuses on trying to help them to build them, rather than punishing them for a lack of them is the most restorative, healing and effective approach. No other discipline methods are going to be successful with these children until these gaps are plugged. Behavioural interventions that focus on the SEL skills and cultural elements of education, actively involving children, are effective in improving student mental health,[29] but also that of staff, and research has shown that children's perception of their teachers' happiness has a significant correlation with their attitude and motivation at school.[30]

Returning to the idea of plugging gaps and meeting unmet

needs, with an emphasis on SEL, American clinical psychologist Dr Ross Greene is known for his Collaborative & Proactive Solutions (CPS) approach to child behaviour. CPS centres on the belief that children are trying their best and that difficult behaviour occurs when what is asked or expected of them is beyond their abilities. Instead of blaming the child for the behaviour and punishing or rewarding them in an attempt to externally motivate them to do better, the CPS approach asks: why are these children struggling? And what unmet needs do they have? As Greene himself says in his book *Lost at School: Why Our Kids with Behavioral Challenges are Falling Through the Cracks and How We Can Help Them*:

> The vast majority of challenging kids already know how we want them to behave. They know they're supposed to do what they're told. They know they're not supposed to disrupt the learning of their classmates or run out of the school when they're upset or embarrassed. And they know they're not supposed to hit people, swear, or call out in class. So, they don't need us to put lots of effort into teaching them how we want them to behave. And while this may be hard to believe, most challenging kids already want to behave the right way. They don't need us to continue giving them stickers, depriving them of recess, or suspending them from school; they're already motivated. They need something else from us.[31]

Greene's work encourages parents, teachers and childcare workers to use an approach to behaviour which focuses on collaborative problem solving – working with children to understand their needs and missing skills – in order that they can be better regulated and behave in the way that is desired.

In addition to adopting Greene's CPS model, an anti-childist education system would be fully understanding and accommodating of all special educational needs and disabilities (SEND).

There would be proper SEND funding, far shorter waiting times for diagnosis and genuine support, rather than an attempt to tick boxes and protect against legal action. Finally, all adults who work with children would have a thorough understanding of SEND conditions and appropriate expectations of behaviour, based upon children's neurological differences. Children with SEND would not be expected to behave in the same way as other children; they would be handled with equity, not equality, in order that their treatment was truly fair.

SEND children are arguably the biggest victims of childism in our education system today. A seismic shift in the way they are viewed in education, especially with behaviour control, would make an enormous difference to them and their families.

Of course, the Thrive, SEL and CPS approaches to behaviour management all require significant time from teaching staff – something that is rarely available while they work in the current system. Teachers will repeatedly say that they cannot adopt more relationship-focused, collaborative techniques because they simply do not have the time to invest, nor the time needed for them to work. Instead, they will often resort to outdated control- and coercion-based methods, which make everybody feel worse, because the pressures of their job mean that they need a 'quick fix'.

The answer here is the transformation that Sir Ken Robinson claims is so desperately needed. This needs to be started by us, the people, the parents and the teaching staff, and our governments need to understand how urgently this dramatic change is needed. A radical change to our education system would save millions, both in cash terms and in lives, however the results would not be seen immediately, and sadly, long-term vision is not something most politicians possess currently. An anti-childist society would once again need to start with an anti-childist government.

The impact of anti-childist mental-health support

Anti-childist methods of parenting and education would undoubtedly have a positive effect on children's mental health, but can you imagine the additional impact of an anti-childist mental-health system for children and adolescents? What would that look like?

Well, to start with it would be properly funded, with a budget uniquely for child mental health support, not a small share of adult services. All children who need mental health support would receive it, rather than playing a lottery of whether they are considered severe enough to receive help, or being fortunate enough to have parents who can afford private treatment.

Staff would be well paid and well supported, waiting lists would be drastically reduced and children needing emergency care would be seen within a few days, not weeks or months. Early intervention would become standard, not just a buzz phrase used to generate good publicity. Care would be holistic and spread across different areas of the community, including schools and primary-care physicians, with specialists trained in child mental health in all settings where children spend time. There would also be a decent understanding of the true extent and incidence of child mental-health issues in society – something that is currently lacking.[32]

The transition from child and adolescent mental-health support (CAMHS) to adult mental-health support would be as seamless as possible, thoroughly explained and take place at the right pace for each child, so that no one falls through the cracks or finds the experience traumatic, as is sadly often the case.[33] Most importantly, children's voices would be heard and listened to.

Finally, all adults would be aware of the importance of child mental health and work to nurture and support it.

Aside from saving significant amounts of money, an anti-childist mental-health support system would help children to reach their full potential and become happier, more secure, adults who will, in time, become parents themselves.

Good mental health for future generations starts with caring for our children's mental health today. An anti-childist approach to this would have a significantly positive impact on adult mental health. We would have a generation of adults who are more emotionally regulated, with more positive relationships, and who would be more likely to raise children with good emotion-regulation skills. We wouldn't only create a better world for our children, but for us too. We would all be happier.

I'd like to end this chapter with the words of cultural anthropologist Margaret Mead, who said: 'Never doubt that a small group of thoughtful, committed citizens can change the world. Indeed, it is the only thing that ever has.' It *is* possible for us to end childism and change the world for our own children and the children of the future – we all have that power within us – we just have to believe that we can. We just have to start.

Chapter 8

'It Never Did Me Any Harm!'

People raised on love see things differently than
those raised on survival.

Joy Marino, **author**

'Well, it must be OK, because it never did me any harm!' How
has this become the benchmark by which we measure childcare
methods? Subjective statements made by those who may not
understand child psychology or be able to cite any research to
back their claims. I often think that the person uttering this statement clearly was harmed in some way as a child, and now exhibits
the very traits we know that outdated, childist, childcare methods
can cause. A person who believes that childist methods are acceptable may well have grown up in an environment where their
feelings were manipulated by adults, their childhood dominated
by fear, control and coercion. And it takes a level of empathy,
emotional maturity and comfort with examining memories to be
able to say, 'Actually, I don't think I was treated very well.'

So, how do you encourage people to open their minds to the
harm that childism causes? The most obvious approach seems to
be to inundate the person with articles, research findings and the
like. This, however, is futile because you are dealing with years of
conditioning and inherited beliefs. It takes a lot more than this
to open minds. The position to start, however rude, dismissive, or

patronising the person, is from one of empathy. We have to start with asking, 'What happened to you in childhood to make you believe this to be true?'

Why people dismiss the idea of childism

People's reasons for dismissal of childism as a concept or denial that discipline or sleep-training methods are overly harsh vary; however, almost all are rooted in their upbringing. Quite simply, a lot of us weren't treated very well when we were children. Here, I'm not talking about blaming or shaming our parents, and I'm also not suggesting that everybody had a miserable childhood. Far from it, we can have the happiest of memories, love our parents deeply and consider them to have been good parents, but still have experienced discrimination and poor treatment as children. Some people are aware of the childism they were on the receiving end of, while others are either unaware or prefer to ignore it. What might lie behind the thinking of those who will not denounce childism?

Cognitive dissonance

In the 1950s, psychologist Leon Festinger introduced the term cognitive dissonance to describe a scenario in which an individual's beliefs about something are challenged and the challenging information makes them feel too uncomfortable to deal with it. This causes them to reject the new information in an attempt to restore psychological homeostasis. In his book *A Theory of Cognitive Dissonance* Festinger says: 'A man with a conviction is a hard man to change. Tell him you disagree and he turns away.

Show him facts or figures and he questions your sources. Appeal to logic and he fails to see your point.'[1] Cognitive dissonance means it is pointless trying to back up your argument with research, facts and quotes because the person will dismiss them all. Festinger goes on to say: 'The existence of dissonance, being psychologically uncomfortable, will motivate the person to try to reduce the dissonance and achieve consonance. When dissonance is present, in addition to trying to reduce it, the person will actively avoid situations and information which would likely increase the dissonance.'[2]

It is incredibly frustrating having a conversation about overly harsh discipline, sleep training or other discrimination of children with somebody who is struggling with cognitive dissonance. Sadly, its very presence indicates a huge inner emotional turmoil. If the information presented didn't trigger the person in question, there would be no dissonance. As children, we are wired for connection and attachment with our parents and carers, and if we don't get the nurturance and support we need, our brains switch to protection mode and we move towards merely surviving. Cognitive dissonance is a symptom of somebody who has grown in survival mode and who is unwittingly demonstrating the harm caused by the very thing they claim to support.

The unconscious need to be in control

For many adults who have experienced stressful, hurtful or harsh treatment in childhood, the unconscious drive to be in control of their own children makes them believe that this is how the adult–child relationship should look. Adults will often subconsciously try to regain control in situations with their children where they feel powerless, a common example being backchat or rudeness and disobedience. The control that the adults subconsciously desire is often sought via harsh discipline methods, where the balance of power is always tipped in their favour. Once the power is restored to them, they feel at ease and like the grown-ups in the situation once again. Someone who was used to feeling controlled as a child, and fearful of the adults who cared for them, is likely to have formed the belief that the child's place is one of no power, with respect for elders always demanded. They will therefore inform a conviction that as an adult they should be in control and they will back this with the statement 'It didn't do me any harm'.

The stiff upper lip

We discussed in Chapters 1–3 how most common parenting methods focus on training children to be quiet, whether in the daytime, when they are put in time out, or at night-time, when they are left to cry to (supposedly) improve their sleep. While the child's quietness makes things easier for adults and the perception is that they have learned how to behave/sleep, this is usually not the case. Rather, the child has learned, through a process of conditioning, to internalise their feelings; they know that their parent or carer does not give them the help and support they need when they are struggling, so they learn to suppress their cries and any verbalisation of their emotions. Children are so often deemed to be 'good' when they are quiet and obedient, but the 'good' child is often one who has learned to suppress their feelings to keep their parent or carer happy.

What are the consequences of this stiff-upper-lip approach? While those who proclaim 'it never did me harm' would likely say that children need to be more resilient and stop being 'snowflakes', their actions suggest that they may have many bottled-up feelings from their own childhoods. I refer to this as emotional constipation – the inability to feel buried emotions, making them powerless to release them. This lack of release is usually coupled with a good dose of cognitive dissonance (see above), which means the individual usually treats any talk of emotions with disdain.

Fawning

You are probably aware of the fight-flight-or-freeze stress response. When a person is faced with an event that they perceive to be dangerous or threatening in some way, their body responds with a chain of chemical and physiological reactions. These will either ready them to run quickly from the threat (flight), stay and fight their corner (fight) or remain temporarily frozen in fear, unable to move or respond verbally (freeze). But there is a fourth stress response that few are aware of: fawning. Named by psychotherapist Pete Walker, the fawn stress response causes individuals to become chronic people pleasers. When they feel threatened, either physically or verbally, instead of running or fighting back, they seek to placate the person threatening them. Those who fawn in response to threats will take a submissive approach, yielding to the other person and voluntarily giving away their power. In time, they can come to believe that they are, in fact, the problem, freely giving away control as a way to avoid conflict.

The fawning approach is common in the adult–child relationship. Adults naturally hold more power over children who need their parents' love in order to maintain attachment and to be kept safe. Fawning is a survival strategy: a child's brain develops coping strategies to preserve the relationship with their parents and to be able to function with the constant threat they feel under when treated harshly. This pattern often continues into adulthood and the 'childhood fawn' becomes a chronic adult people pleaser, with low self-esteem and unbalanced power in their relationships. The fawning towards their parents continues, too, with individuals growing to justify their parents' actions ('It never did me any harm') in the genuine belief that they deserved the harsh treatment they received.

Dissociation

Dissociation falls under the 'freeze' banner of the stress response. It happens when an individual finds a scenario too stressful to deal with, so they switch off and zone out mentally and physically. The freeze response causes them to feel numb, which is preferable to the fear and anxiety felt if they engage with either the fight or flight response instead. To help with dissociating from the pain they might feel, whether emotional or physical, an individual will often distract themselves with food (comfort eating), alcohol or getting lost in fictional books, TV shows or computer games. These habits begin as an attempt to 'space out' and take their mind off the threat, but they can often form a new habit that becomes too painful for them to deal with.

Dissociation in childhood can occur because of a difficult parent–child relationship, where the child lives under constant threat of punishment and harsh treatment, or they are left with their difficult emotions by an emotionally uninvolved parent. The child learns to dissociate from not only specific stressful situations but also, ultimately, from their childhood altogether – often they will have few childhood memories and will struggle to recollect events when others discuss them. As well as forgetting a chunk of their childhood, dissociation can also cause them to forget the harsh treatment from their parents and any damage this may have caused. Hence the claim, 'It never did me any harm'.

Stockholm Syndrome

Stockholm Syndrome is named after a bank robbery that occurred in Stockholm, Sweden in the early 1970s. As part of the robbery, four hostages were taken and held by the robbers for almost a week. The hostages were used as human shields by the thieves, ensuring that if police attempted to capture them, that the hostages would die first. The trauma of this treatment led the hostages to begin to form attachments to their captors, resulting in them being uncooperative during police hostage release negotiations and refusing to give evidence to the police when they were finally freed in an attempt to protect their captors. One of the hostages kept in touch with the man who masterminded the robbery, meeting several times, even becoming friends.

Psychologists use the term Stockholm Syndrome to describe the relationship between a person inflicting abuse (physical or psychological, or both) and their victim. The victim bonds with their abuser in a process known as trauma bonding, and will often become their loudest cheerleader, denying any abuse. They will latch on to any small kindnesses on the part of the abuser, offering these up as supposed proof of good character, and will view them with empathy, believing that they are justified in their actions.

Trauma bonding occurs within the parent–child relationship, when children are treated harshly, but are the first to stand up for their parents, desperate to preserve the bond between them. A child does not have to have been legally abused for this to take place; it is a common response among those who were spanked as children, for example, and, yet again, it underpins 'it-never-did-me-any-harm' thinking.

Groupthink

Groupthink is a term used to describe a psychological phenomenon in which people unconsciously seek to create harmony and keep the peace within a group by not speaking out against the views it seems to hold. These groups can take many forms, from work colleagues to friends or family members.

If those raised in families that use harsh childcare methods believe that all other family members (including siblings, parents, grandparents and cousins) are OK with them, it is unlikely that they will speak up.

Groupthink is common on social media, where individuals self-identify as part of a group and continue to uphold its common belief, regardless of their opinions. Think about spanking debates you may have seen online, and the fierce defending of an idea by those who identify with pro-spanking movements and statements of 'it never did me any harm'.

Groupthink carries with it huge levels of peer pressure, an inherent wariness and dislike of strangers or those with opposing opinions and a mistaken belief that all members of a group are in total agreement. Groupthink is such that it is almost impossible to get through to individuals, because it doesn't just mean they will have to change their own views, it also means that their unofficial membership of the group will be broken, which brings with it all sorts of feelings of vulnerability that the individual does not want.

Genuine belief that it didn't harm them

There is always the possibility that some adults may have no idea that they have been harmed by harsh parenting methods. To recognise any harm requires a level of self-awareness and introspection that many just don't have. We all know some-body who is clearly not OK but considers that there is absolutely nothing wrong with them or their beliefs. Sometimes only the knowledge, experience and expertise of mental-health profession-als can pinpoint the harm that has been done to somebody, and the views of the lay person are simply not informed enough for them to self-diagnose.

In some cases, people just do not recognise that events from their own childhoods were traumatic. Maybe they did not find them so, although many others would have done. However, just because they did not experience trauma at the time, it doesn't mean that they were untouched by the experiences. Additionally, as children, we are often not aware of unjust treatment; we do not realise that the way we were treated was wrong and it can take many years, until some point in adulthood, before we do. I have often spoken to older individuals who just do not realise that what they experienced as children actually verged on neglect and abuse – so when they say 'It never did me any harm' they genuinely believe it.

Ad hominem

While not an excuse for saying 'it never did me any harm', I think it's important that we talk about *ad hominem* attacks at this point – because if you speak out about childism, this is something you will face, and being prepared will help to take the edge off it when it happens.

Ad hominem, which is Latin for 'to the person', occurs when an individual is unable to argue with the logic and rationale behind someone's argument, and instead criticises the individual themselves. This can take the form of attacking their perceived expertise and qualifications (again, in an attempt to refute their argument), but often resorts to hitting out against the person's morals, abilities or appearance. Common *ad hominem* attacks I receive when I speak about childism centre on me not knowing what I'm talking about, being a busybody do-gooder, being 'a Karen' and being an unattractive middle-aged woman. One *Daily Mail* reader comment proclaimed that I clearly wasn't getting any sex and that was why I was so worked up about adults not hitting children.

The interesting thing about *ad hominem* attacks is that when they happen, you know the attacker is unable to argue with your point, in essence proving you are correct. As author Nassim Nicholas Taleb says in his book *The Black Swan*: 'An *ad hominem* attack against an intellectual, not against an idea, is highly flattering. It indicates that the person does not have anything intelligent to say about your message.'

When research shows harsh childhood treatment does cause harm

The big difference in talking about childism today and not fifty or a hundred years ago is that science can now prove that harsh treatment in childhood does indeed cause harm. A wealth of scientific evidence, study findings, brain scans and more prove the impact of childhood in shaping who we become as adults and how trauma travels through generations. While the science deniers cling on to the idea that they weren't harmed in any way, using *ad hominem* attacks ('Scientists don't know what they're talking about; they just make it all up') and claiming that their own subjective experience proves all the data wrong, empirical evidence tells a different story.

Research has found that childhood trauma has long-lasting psychological impacts. For instance, those people who were on the receiving end of harsh treatment as children find it harder to regulate their own emotions and control impulsive behaviours as adults.[3] Studies show that traumatic experiences in infancy can impact the development of the HPA (hypothalamic-pituitary-adrenal) axis, a major neuroendocrine system, which helps to regulate how our bodies respond to stress.[4] The HPA axis is shaped by early life experiences, and trauma in the early years can result in imbalances in the secretion of stress hormones, such as cortisol, into adulthood.

The impact of our early years can – and does – shape who we become as adults, including our preferred parenting styles. Research has found that those who are drawn to harsher styles of discipline display reduced levels of humility and empathy and more antisocial traits than those who prefer a more nurturing style.[5] This gravitation towards authoritarian and harmful parenting practices, likely caused by being raised in a similar environment themselves, creates a cascade of cycles of trauma, whereby the same childism is passed down from generation to generation, literally altering the wiring in the brains of some families.[6]

We know that maternal trauma is linked to what scientists refer to as 'negative parenting outcomes'.[7] Mothers who were themselves traumatised as a child are more likely to engage in over-punitive parenting, corporal punishment and verbally abusive aggression aimed at their children. Sadly, many of these mothers are unaware that they are repeating generational patterns of trauma; they simply find themselves in a difficult position, with unruly, demanding children, who make them feel out of control, triggering their own internal distress and emotions. In this case, neither parent nor child wins. The mothers find themselves in a perpetual state of discomfort, living out their own childhood triggers, while unintentionally passing them on to the next generation. Sometimes they may try to avoid creating the same situations they lived through as a child but can struggle with their child's attachment needs for them and feel out of control and helpless as the child grows.

This battle for control between parent and child and the parent's need to feel emotional equilibrium can lead to more overly harsh or, sometimes, dissociative behaviour, where the parent withdraws their love and attention from the child. The child then begins to internalise their emotions because they cannot trust their parent to support and help them. And a new cycle begins when, one day, that 'emotionally constipated' child has their own children with their own big emotions.

What of those who were punished physically as children? Does this influence their views on corporal punishment? Research tells us that indeed it does.[8] Those who were hit by their own parents or carers as children are significantly more likely to use the same behaviours when they become parents. Although these individuals claim that the spanking, smacking, tapping and so on that they experienced as children 'never did me any harm', the fact that they now believe it is OK to hit vulnerable children is surely evidence enough that it has influenced them. A meta-analysis of over 160,000 children found that being hit as a child increased the likelihood of the child growing to develop:[9]

- aggressive behaviour
- mental-health problems
- alcohol or substance abuse
- lower self-regulation abilities
- impaired cognitive abilities
- antisocial behaviour
- internalisation of emotions.

The research also found that if children were hit by their parents, they were more likely to have been on the receiving end of other harsh discipline methods, such as yelling, shaming, excluding and illogical consequences. This all seems like evidence of harm to me.

What's behind the 'anti-woke' agenda?

In the last few years there has been increasing opposition to what is termed the 'woke agenda'. *The Cambridge Dictionary* defines 'woke' as 'aware, especially of social problems such as racism and inequality', while agenda is defined as 'a list of aims or possible future achievements'. From this, we have to presume that a 'woke agenda' is a list of aims, based on awareness of social inequality. That sounds pretty good to me, especially if we throw childism into the mix. Only most people don't seem to use the words in a positive context; instead, 'woke' is used as a slur, with an 'agenda' being viewed as a sinister plot, akin to a conspiracy, the suggestion being that armies of crazy new-age liberals are banding together to take over the world with their wacky ideas, threatening the very existence of normal people and their traditional lives. Others believe that 'woke' is part of a grand masterplan, spearheaded by the Rothschilds, or Klaus Schwab and the World Economic Forum, to strategically disassemble society as it stands currently, in order to throw us into a new, unwanted, industrial revolution. 'Woke' is something that is feared, reviled, ridiculed, and dismissed, especially by those whose beliefs fit in with the historical childcare experts and their patriarchy. Woke threatens outdated discriminatory views and, instead of rationally discussing work to try to rid the world of inequality and discrimination, arguments quickly descend into *ad hominem*.

Another thing that might underpin the views of those who are anti-woke is the feeling of a loss of control in a changing world. For those born half a century ago or more, societal change and shifts in viewpoints can undoubtedly prove unsettling. Imagine feeling sure of your views, with a good amount of groupthink in your peer circles, and then seeing constant reports challenging your beliefs. It would be natural to try to dismiss the new view-points as a form of self-preservation and an attempt to restore the balance of power. Research has shown that parents who believe their children hold more power than them in difficult situations are more likely to believe that they are manipulative.[10] These beliefs make the parents feel threatened and in a subconscious attempt to restore power and control, they tend to become more hostile and aggressive towards their children. I do wonder if there is an element of this same behaviour pattern occurring when the childcare experts of previous generations feel the need to verbally attack younger generations, as a subconscious way of feeling more in control in an ever changing world? Similarly, those born in an era where scientific research into the impact of parenting methods was lacking, are more likely to have less informed expectations of child behaviour. If they do not understand stages of normal child development, it is understandable that they believe that children today are 'out of control', 'unruly' and 'disrespectful'. The natural next step, based on these incorrect assumptions, is that 'the parents of today' are not doing a very good job with their children. The obvious point to blame here is 'wokeness' and so-called gentle and respectful parenting styles, which are often dismissed as 'lazy', 'neglectful' and 'permissive'. Again, this isn't about blame, I truly believe that those who spearhead the anti-woke agenda should be viewed with empathy. We should be asking, 'What happened to you when you were a child to make you think this?' Meeting their slurs with our own is never going to change anything; only understanding will.

I'd like to end this chapter by answering three questions I am always asked when I speak of intergenerational cycles of trauma and childism and tackling the 'it-never-did-me-any-harm' people.

1. **How do we deal with our own triggers, so we can be less childist ourselves?** We must begin by looking inwards. What happened to you in your own childhood

that could have had an impact on how you view the behaviour of your child or children? Might you hold subconscious childist beliefs, thinking that adults should hold power over children, or that children shouldn't have the same rights as adults because they are somehow less than them? Do you identify with any of the concepts in this chapter – dissociation, fawning or Stockholm Syndrome, for example?

It doesn't matter how happy your childhood was, or how wonderful your parents were – you still grew up in a world that didn't treat you very well. If something triggers you with your own children, it is highly likely that a raw nerve from your own childhood has been hit. The way forward here is taking some time to connect with your inner child (we will talk about this more in the next chapter) – to close your eyes and travel back a few decades and recognise the childism that you faced. This work also involves a huge amount of forgiveness. I have stated repeatedly that talking about childism isn't about blaming our parents and grandparents, schoolteachers or other carers, because, in turn, each of them was also affected by childism. It's about having empathy and understanding for everybody and realising that, as former children, we all carry a little collective trauma with us and for that we need to treat ourselves kindly, patiently and with grace.

2. **What do you do when you can't change somebody's mind?** I hope you now understand a little more about why it's not as easy as simply sending somebody an online article about gentle parenting or a research study if they don't agree with your parenting, or if you are trying to change childist viewpoints. Their beliefs and those statements are based on years of conditioning, and you are absolutely not going to undo them all

overnight, nor, in all likelihood, in this lifetime. What you can do, however, is to have the same empathy for others, especially those from older generations, as you wish to show yourself and your children. Again, don't think, 'What's wrong with you? Why are you like this?' – think, 'What happened to you? What did you have to go through as a child yourself to make you feel this way?' Focus on connection, empathy and understanding, and when you are ready to have a conversation, focus on emotions and something called 'mind-mindedness'. Mind-mindedness is a parenting approach which puts the adult in the shoes of the child, asking, 'Why are they behaving like this? How are they feeling? How would I feel in their situation? What would I have needed as a child myself?' In essence, mind-mindedness is what I am suggesting you practise with adults who hold childist views, and it is the only approach that may slowly chip away at their self-protective armour, allowing them to begin to see things through anti-childist eyes.

3. **Are all those from previous generations childist?**
   No. While everybody has faced childism to a degree, there are many who are naturally anti-childist and who fiercely stand up for the rights of children, some having spearheaded change. (Remember Eglantyne Jebb who founded Save the Children – see page 18) Similarly, those from younger generations can be equally as childist as older people, or more so. Being anti-childist is about working together to heal ourselves, for a more equitable future for our children. There is no space for blame or shame in this work. Remember, we were all raised in a childist society – but some of us just don't realise it yet, and arguably deserve more patience and kinder treatment than those who are 'awake'.

Talk of society is a good place to end this chapter because working with others is an important step towards ushering in an anti-childist movement. We can work independently to change our own thought patterns and beliefs, but we can't bring about on our own the paradigm shift that is necessary to create a society that genuinely embraces the rights of children – we need to work with others to do that. In the next chapter, we will explore this idea and more, as we talk about how to become a cycle breaker and an advocate for children.

Chapter 9

How to Be a Cycle Breaker

If you can't run, then walk. If you can't walk,
then crawl, but whatever you do, you have to
keep moving forward.

MARTIN LUTHER KING JR,
American Baptist minister
and civil-rights activist

I wonder how you feel having read the first eight chapters of this book. Do you believe that childism exists in our society? Can you remember incidences of childism from your own childhood? Do you feel compelled to try to make a change for the sake of your own children?

If you would like to be a cycle breaker, then this chapter is for you. The question is where to start? Well, it always starts with us.

As I mentioned much earlier, I have written fourteen books about parenting to date and, despite what many would believe given the titles and back-cover blurbs, every single one of them is about changing adults, not children. Gentle (or authoritative) parenting places its focus on the behaviour of adults (as opposed to authoritarian parenting, which focuses on trying to change the behaviour of children). Tackling childism is no different from parenting conundrums. And, as I said, it starts with us.

The very first step is pausing to consider how we ourselves

have been impacted by childism – acknowledging that we carry unconscious biases and beliefs, and understanding that much of our behaviour is conditioned by the way we were treated in childhood by adults, including our own parents. We have to break through the cognitive dissonance (see page 153) and realise that a lot of the treatment we received as children *did* do us harm. Psychologists tend to call this work 'inner-child healing'. As the name suggests, it means healing the child within us, so that we do not carry our hurt into the next generation. It means recognising and accepting that we were treated harshly as children, so we can break the cycle of childism.

How to heal your inner child

You will often hear therapists talking about 'doing the work', but what exactly is the work and how do you do it? In short, it has six main parts:

1. Realising the harm caused
2. Connecting with our inner child
3. Making peace with our past and those in it
4. Putting boundaries in place to protect ourselves in the future
5. Working on our emotion regulation
6. Making community connections

Let's look at each of these in more detail.

Realising the harm caused

It is impossible for adults to become allies for children and campaign to reduce childism if they do not understand the harm it caused them as children. Growing up in a childist society has impacted every one of us. Our upbringings shape our world view, create our belief systems and unconsciously guide our actions when we become parents.

Perhaps you find yourself with low tolerance for normal but testing child behaviour? Perhaps you feel the need to discipline your child harshly to 'teach them a lesson' when they seemingly disrespect you. Or perhaps you somehow believe that child rights are different from human rights? None of these is your fault. Neither do they make you a bad person or somehow a poor parent. We are all products of our own childhoods. I think acknowledging the harmful and hurtful treatment we were on the receiving end of as children is perhaps the hardest step to becoming anti-childist, but it is also the most important one. We have to start with realising and accepting that childism *did* do us harm.

To break the cycle of childism, therefore, we first have to free ourselves of the biased thoughts and discriminatory beliefs we hold. To be better allies to children, we also have to recognise the privilege we hold, simply by being adults. Privilege in this sense doesn't mean that we are always treated well by others or that we are not discriminated against in other ways; it simply means, in this case, that now we are adults, we are no longer subjected to childism. There is power in this privilege, and we can use it to be a force for good and change. But we have to start by acknowledging it.

Connecting with our inner child

Growing up in a childist society often meant that we had to hide and bury our emotions as children, it often meant that we were poorly treated by those who were meant to protect and love us most. The harsh treatment we experienced may have led us to develop a fawning, people-pleasing stress response. Perhaps it caused us to dissociate a little from our childhoods, perhaps we experienced Stockholm Syndrome as a way to protect ourselves, or maybe we grew to make excuses for our parents and carers, believing that somehow, we were not worthy of better treatment, and deserved their punishments. All of this causes wounds to our psyche. Hurt people hurt people, and in order to break the cycle of childism we have to start with healing ourselves, or more specifically – our inner children.

Somewhere deep inside us all is a child, desperate for somebody to listen to them, to support them and to tell them all the things they wish they had heard growing up. The simplest way to help this inner child is to connect with them by re-parenting ourselves. What does that look like? Your self-talk needs to adopt a nurturing, accepting voice, rather than the self-critical one so many of us are used to. It means revisiting painful memories and acknowledging the child you once were and the needs you had. It means metaphorically giving yourself a hug and telling yourself that you deserved better. It was never your fault. You are 'worth it', and you were not responsible for the emotions of those who projected their dysregulated feelings on to you.

Inner-child healing also involves getting back in touch with those things you enjoyed as a child, such as play and creativity. What did you like doing? What made you laugh? What made you happy? Are these things still in your life? Maybe you enjoyed painting or drawing, cycling or dancing, making music, pretending and acting? Or maybe daydreaming or writing stories? As adults, amid the busyness and demands of daily living, we so often forget who we really are, but taking time to reconnect with the joys of inner childhood can make us feel truly whole again.

Making peace with our past and those in it

I have mentioned several times already that inner-child work and the process of becoming anti-childist do not constitute a blame game. It is not about shaming or confronting our parents and carers. It is not about feelings of anger, regret or resentment. Quite the contrary, in fact – it is about making peace with our pasts and using the childism we faced to fuel our desire to change. Again, this work is not about falling out with our elders. We must remember that they were victims of childism, too. In fact, it's likely that the childism they faced was much more severe. If your parents and grandparents grew up around the time of the First or Second World War, or the decade or two that followed, they were likely on the receiving end of childcare methods that came straight from the mouths of the historical childcare experts. They may well have been harmed a lot, even if they are not in a place to recognise or admit it. And perhaps they never will, which is OK, because it's likely the cognitive dissonance they wear as a shield against any pain is too strong.

Being anti-childist doesn't necessarily mean that we need to convert everybody, particularly those from older generations. Of course, some of our parents and grandparents will already be fiercely anti-childist, maybe because they have acknowledged the treatment they received as children, or perhaps because they are among the lucky few who grew up with already anti-childist parents. Either way, it doesn't matter, because to break the cycle we need to focus on future actions and positive steps we can take to change, not dwelling on toxic memories and relationships.

Putting boundaries in place to protect us in the future

Following on from the previous point, if you are struggling with your own upbringing having read this book, and your parents and carers are not open to discussion, then boundaries are important to protect you. If you feel that your relationship with your parents may drag you down and negatively impact the relationship you have with your own children and there is no way to rectify it, then it is OK for you to distance yourself from them physically and emotionally.

It's important to say 'no' to things that may disturb your peace and leach negativity into other areas of your life. It's OK to not have conversations that you know will make you feel angry and frustrated. It's also OK to say 'no' to other things that make you feel stretched in different directions. It's likely you are a better parent and a better ally if you are choosy about what you take on and what you commit to. Having boundaries and accepting your limits is an important step if you want to feel calmer and have enough energy to really focus on raising your children in an anti-childist way or campaign for better treatment for others. You also do not have to join every argument or debate you are invited to, nor do you have to get involved with every childism-related discussion on the Internet. Sometimes protecting your peace and walking away is a far better choice.

Working on our emotion regulation

Just as being a cycle breaker is not about blaming or shaming others, the same is true of yourself. We tend to be harder on ourselves than anybody else, and it's important to lighten this load if you want to focus on being anti-childist. Every single parent and carer has repeated childist cycles of discipline, sleep training, privacy invasions or similar with their children or children in their care. There will be many things you have said or done to your children or to others' that you'll likely cringe at having read this book – and that's OK. But to move forwards and make meaningful change, you have to start with being gracious and forgiving yourself for mistakes made when you either didn't know better or life got in the way of your good intentions.

Being a cycle breaker is not about being perfect. Far from it. It's about recognising the conditioning we have experienced and moments when we were struggling, and realising that it's not our fault. It's about taking small but consistent steps towards change. It's about starting and trying and realising that we are good enough, and that's all that it takes.

In my book *How to be a Calm Parent* I talk about the importance of focusing on our own emotions and learning to regulate them to be a calmer parent. Despite our best intentions there are always going to be moments when we are unable to be the parents we want to be. Childist parenting methods mean that many of us were raised in a way that negatively impacted our ability to regulate our own emotions. In fact, this lack of adult self-regulation skills is perhaps both the hardest and most damaging element in all relationships, not just parent–child ones.

The good news here is that it is possible to improve self-regulation skills. Again, this starts with accepting our feelings, whatever they are. No feelings are good, no feelings are bad; they just are – a concept known as 'emodiversity'. Rather than feeling bad or naughty for having big emotions, such as anger and jealousy, as we did as children, we need, as adults, to acknowledge and accept them. What matters now is what we do with these emotions and how we handle them. In moments when we feel our self-regulation slipping, then we should apologise to those who are on the receiving end of our dysregulation. In *How to be a Calm Parent* I talk about the importance of apologising to children:

... it's OK to make mistakes as a parent, so long as we understand how our children feel and help them to feel better if
(or should I say 'when') we upset them. This is often referred
to as the rupture–repair cycle. When we inevitably lose our
temper and yell at our children, we cause a rupture in our
relationship with them, but our attunement with them allows
us to see the hurt we have caused and leads us to repair the
rupture, through holding space and containing the emotions
and behaviour that result in our children, and through gentle
words and touch. I prefer to call this effect the holler-and-heal
cycle, because, even when I do holler and yell, I am reminded
that we can still heal. I can make things right; all is not lost.
Healing is always possible. Children are more resilient than
we think, especially if we apologise and reconnect, or heal,
after losing control ... When I have the holler-and-heal conversation with parents, I'm always asked 'but how do you
apologise to your children?' We live in a culture where very
few adults apologise to children. It's likely that we weren't
apologised to during our own childhoods, especially if we
were raised with a belief (held by many) that 'the adult is
always right'. Only they're not. Adults mess up all the time.
We apologise to other adults, why wouldn't we apologise to
children? I actually believe it is vitally important we mess up
as parents, because if we didn't, we would have no reason to
apologise to our children and therefore our children would
never learn what to do when they make their own mistakes
and need to apologise to others. It's a strange notion indeed
that adults frequently force children to apologise for their
misdeeds without ever having been on the receiving end of
an apology from an adult. How do we expect them to learn?
If we want to raise children who are able to apologise – and
genuinely mean what they say – we have to apologise to them,
and to do that we have to screw up first.

Learning to apologise to children when we mess up is one of the most important steps we can all take towards becoming anti-childist and breaking the cycle of discrimination of children. Those steps don't have to be huge – in fact it's better that they're not because that way we avoid burnout. As the immensely wise Martin Luther King Junior said, quoted at the beginning of this chapter: 'If you can't run, then walk. If you can't walk, then crawl, but whatever you do, you have to keep moving forward.'

Making community connections

Having begun your work with self-awareness and self-change, the next step towards a societal paradigm shift is to grow a grass-roots movement of committed citizens who work together with a common goal of breaking the cycle of childism.

Linking up with people who understand you and who share your ideals can not only help to further your goals, but also keep you feeling strong while you set about achieving them. Becoming anti-childist in a childist society means that you will be verbally attacked, you will be on the receiving end of groupthink and *ad hominem* attacks (see pages 160–61) and this can, understandably, make you feel stressed, saddened and even question if it is worth carrying on. When you have support from others, the group can uplift and inspire you in ways that you will not experience alone.

How do you link up with others? Forming communities of like-minded people is easier today than it ever has been because we have the Internet. While it would be wonderful to meet up in person, the easiest starting point is meeting online. Search for discussion groups about social change, social activism, gentle parenting and respectful parenting, and if none suits you, consider starting your own. In time, it is possible to make local connections and arrange meet-ups.

Your meet-ups may then grow to include:

- meetings to discuss anti-childism thoughts and activities
- book groups to discuss relevant and related topics and ideas
- anti-childist playgroups, meeting with other parents and their babies and toddlers
- social media pages or handles, where you share your thoughts to a wider audience
- joining the school parent–teacher association to drip feed anti-childist thoughts into school events and policies
- starting an anti-childist home education group if school is not for you.

Being a cycle breaker is hard to do alone, but when you have the support of other like-minded individuals, it can not only make the work easier but also give you a shared sense of purpose and motivation.

Ask the children

Article 12 of the UN Convention on the Rights of the Child states: 'Parties shall assure to the child who is capable of forming his or her own views the right to express those views freely in all matters affecting the child, the views of the child being given due weight in accordance with the age and maturity of the child.' One incredibly important way to break the cycle of childism is to give every child the right to expression of their emotions, viewpoints and beliefs, especially relating to issues that directly affect them. This freedom of expression should be taken seriously.

How can we do this? Well, it starts at home. Holding family meetings and asking your children to contribute to family rules, listening to their opinions concerning important decisions such as choosing schools, activities and who they may want to live with when a parental relationship breaks down are all ways to give them a voice.

And what about outside the home? All organisations providing services to children, including schools, would benefit from having a child council or child advisory committee, where children who are effectively stakeholders get an active say in the aims and goals of the organisation and the policies and procedures that affect them.

How can organisations take children's voices more seriously? They could:

- speak to children and really listen to their answers
- hold votes and ballots that children can vote in
- provide feedback boxes and short surveys, where comments can be made completely anonymously
- actively seek consent from children about any activities that may potentially breach their privacy
- seek to form an advisory committee comprising diverse ages, genders, ethnicities and social demographics, so that as many children as possible are represented
- ensure that all forms of research and feedback are written in a way that is accessible to children based upon their age and cognitive abilities
- ensure that children are provided with enough information, imparted in a way that is accessible to them, so that they can make informed decisions and choices
- ensure that at all times children feel they are able to engage in a safe and non-judgemental way, free of patronisation or ridicule.

One important way to ensure that children's voices are heard is to afford them a vote at a younger age. In Chapter 1, we looked at voting ages around the world (see pages 26–27). Reducing the voting age to sixteen would give children more say in their futures and, according to research, would also improve long-term turnout at future elections.[1] Researchers looking at the impact of lowering voting ages in Scotland found that if children are allowed to vote at sixteen, they are more invested in politics, not only in the short term, with significant turnouts at their first opportunity to vote, but also as they get older. Commenting on the results, lead author Dr Jan Eichhorn from the School of Social and Political Science at the University of Edinburgh stated:

> Allowing 16- and 17-year-olds to vote was a good decision taken by the Scottish Parliament. Many younger first-time voters retain a habit of voting and participate in greater numbers than older first-time voters. The findings strengthen the case for enfranchising younger voters across the UK to improve long-term voting behaviour. But more can be done. Making sure all young people receive great civic education that includes learning how to discuss political issues well could help reduce persistent social inequalities in turnout.

Allowing children to vote at sixteen would certainly be in line with Article 12 of the UNCRC and a big step towards reducing childism in society today.

Call out childism

Another way you can be a cycle breaker is to call out any inci-dences of childism you come across. This can not only help to change things moving forwards, but it also lets any children who are with you at the time know that you are on their side and that they have an ally in you. That said, be careful how you approach this, remembering that most people are unaware of it and everyone is a victim of it. Many are not ready to be called out and will respond defensively, with anger, and you may well feel worse. The best thing is to tread carefully, with empathy, aiming to help others to understand and not attacking them verbally, either in person or online.

It seems that on an almost daily basis I am tagged on social media when celebrities or influencers post particularly childist things (usually relating to sleep training or harsh discipline). The thinking behind tagging me, I presume, is so that I can point out what is wrong with the way the person who has posted is treating their children. I would never do this, though. Now and again, I may offer some words of support to the original poster (rather than the one who has tagged me) because I recognise that as parents they are, in all likelihood, doing the best they can with the resources, support and understanding they have. But it is not the time for calling them out publicly or, indeed, privately. In such situations, we need to take a breath, recognise our place of privilege over them, given our awareness and understanding, and remind ourselves that they are trying to do their best.

Supporting parents who are struggling and resorting to harsh parenting techniques may feel counterproductive, but it is always more effective than shaming them. If they feel less angry, less tired and less guilty, they will naturally be less childist and more open to different ways of doing things. What they don't need is to be pulled into a full-on critique of their parenting choices on social media, which is embarrassing for them, and their shutters will come down. As the saying goes, 'You catch more flies with honey than vinegar'. If you consistently show up and support people, they are more likely to listen and ask for help.

Similarly, with older generations, remember that they probably experienced far worse childism than you as a child. They also likely raised their children based upon childist advice they received at the time, often from trusted professionals, so the cognitive dissonance will be strong, and so will groupthink, as mentioned earlier. Call out the childism, but do it gently, with baby steps, and go easy on them. You may not be able to change their minds about everything, but starting with something small and doable can be the catalyst for more change.

Childism should always be challenged in a non-violent way. Don't resort to *ad hominem* attacks. Instead, stay calm and use reasoning; be polite, but persistent. For the world to really embrace the concept of childism and for real, tangible change, those who are anti-childist advocates need to be seen as rational and respectful. If we are seen as a fringe movement of crazy alternative hippies (as is so often suggested) it becomes far easier for people to ignore the actual message and to dismiss the whole argument. Welcome debate and encourage people to think for themselves, not just believe what you tell them. Urge people to approach discussion in a 'mind-minded' way, which involves putting the adult in the shoes of the child when considering a given situation. Thinking about the world from the position of a child on the receiving end of childism is a far more powerful way to debate it than name calling or producing mountains of scientific research.

Finally, we should promote positivity and try to lead by example in our own interactions with children – watching the antithesis of childism in action has a very powerful impact.

Practical ways to be an anti-childist ally

In addition to what we have already discussed in this chapter, there are a few practical things we can all do to raise awareness of childism and break the cycle. As mentioned earlier, coming together as a community is by far the most impactful way to bring about change.

- Write to your MP, encouraging them to look into childism in politics. You could start with one particular issue e.g. childcare funding, school funding or lowering voting ages.
- Start a petition – perhaps to the government or, thinking smaller, to a local council, school, youth group or similar. This can also be sent to your MP.
- Get creative – for instance, if you are into the arts, you could stage a production about childism, write a song about it or make a piece of art.
- Organise a peaceful demonstration or march outside parliament or local council offices, or outside an event or organisation that uses childist practices.
- Sit-ins – if you have been somewhere that disrespected child rights, you could organise a sit-in there, with like-minded people, to show your support to children.
- Volunteer for an organisation that is either directly or indirectly involved in tackling childism (you can find some at the back of this book – see page 209). Volunteering your time, however much you can spare, even just an hour or two per month, can really help them.
- Consider getting involved with politics. Perhaps you could stand for your local council or aim bigger. How wonderful it would be if the leaders of tomorrow were actively anti-childist.

Finally, I'm going to write something I have never done as an author before. I am going to actively ask you to share this book. Tell your friends, family, colleagues and anybody you come across who works with children about it. Ask your library to stock the book. If you have available funds, consider gifting a copy to your local politician. Leave a review online (they really matter!) or recommend the book on your social media or to your book club.

Anything you can do to get the word out would be amazing. You are my community, and I need your help as much as you need mine.

Blueprint for an anti-childist society

In Chapter 7 we discussed what an anti-childist society could look like, but I would like to refine that a little more. I believe that there are ten main principles of an anti-childist society:

1. **Radical acceptance of children and their developmental abilities** This means that we would all understand what behaviour (including sleep) looks like at each age and what children are truly capable of. They would not, therefore, be punished for or trained out of behaviours that are, in fact, in line with their cognitive or physical capabilities and we would instead ask ourselves how best we could support them. Anti-childism must start with a realistic understanding of child development.

2. **Recognition that each child is an individual** We would understand that all children are unique. They all have different strengths, weaknesses, interests and passions. Education curriculums would be designed to support this, and SEND and mental-health support would be far more bespoke, truly meeting the needs of children. We would also not raise children according to routines written by others who have never met them.

3. **Properly funded education** Education would rightly be seen as the most important investment politicians could make. Facilities would be kept in good repair and up to date. Curriculums would be holistic and free of neoliberalism. Teachers would receive remuneration

commensurate with their qualifications and expertise, with working conditions designed to retain staff as much as possible, and we would appreciate the skill and work of teachers and the contribution they make to society.

4. **Properly funded childcare** Funding childcare would be a main priority, with good-quality childcare being affordable for all. Free government childcare places would be appropriately funded, so that providers did not constantly struggle to plug budget holes. Childcare in general would be subsidised for all. Childcare workers would be paid appropriately, in recognition of their qualifications, experience and service to society. In addition, if parents chose to stay at home with their children, there would be financial support for them to do so.

5. **Adult recognition of past trauma** Adults would understand that we were all raised in a childist society and that the treatment we received has likely harmed us in some way, even if we are not consciously aware of it. We would work to undo the impact this has had. Children need adults who have healed their childhood wounds to be generational cycle breakers.

6. **Appreciation that childhood is not a practice for adulthood** We would understand that childhood is its own unique time and should be enjoyed as such. Childhood should not be viewed as a period of intense preparation for adulthood, nor should children be treated harshly in a mistaken attempt to prime them for the difficulties of adult life. Children should be allowed to fully embrace everything that being a child means, including play and free time to explore and create, for no reason other than having fun.

7. **Treating children with the same respect as we would**

an adult Instead of adults demanding respect from children, respect should be seen as something that is given to everybody, including children. Adults should not receive respect just because they demand it from children, and especially not adults who do not first show respect to children.

8. **Giving children a voice – and listening to them** It is a human right to have your voice heard and to have freedom of expression. Children should be allowed to share their views and discuss their own beliefs and should be given a say in activities and organisations that involve them. In addition, the voting age should be lowered to sixteen, to afford children a say in their future by voting for policies that affect them.

9. **Aiming for equity over equality** Treating children equally to adults often means treating them unfairly because children are not the same as adults cognitively or physically. Treating children with equity means giving them the same rights and opportunities as adults but adjusting these to accommodate for child development and how they learn and function best.

10. **Mindful inclusivity** Being anti-childist means being inclusive of all children, but realising that some (such as those from ethnic minorities or those who live in poverty) are likely to face extra discrimination – they should be given the extra help needed to give them the rights they deserve, again treating them with equity over equality.

Deciding to become a cycle breaker, to stand up for the rights of children and denounce society's discrimination of them, is life changing. You will no longer view the world, and the people in it, in the same way. You will be frequently frustrated, sad and angry. Your eyes will be opened to the inequalities in your current and past relationships. You will learn to better understand those dearest to you and, more importantly, those you do not like. Because who we become as adults is mapped out by how we were raised in childhood. Those who seem to be the least likeable in our society are those who need our grace and love the most – because they were likely to have been on the receiving end of the most childism when they were small.

Breaking generational cycles is hard work, sometimes exhausting, and you will bring memories to light that you would rather had stayed buried. Sometimes the fire inside you will burn strong, and you will want to convert the whole world, to make people wake up and see what is happening right in front of them. There will also be times when you'll wonder if you can carry on, questioning the impact of your efforts and the toll they take on you. It can be easy to burn out, to have what therapists call 'compassion fatigue'. This is why you should take your time and work at your own pace. Small steps towards positive change are worth every bit as much as huge gestures. Take time out from the cause entirely if you need to – childism will still be there when you are ready to take up the fight again. Finally, link up with others with similar mindsets, lean on them for support, go to them when you feel you are alone in the world.

You are already making a difference.

The cycle ends with us.

Chapter 10

Anti-childism Myth Busting

If you're going to call someone a snowflake
because they believe in a different policy than
you, you might want to look in the mirror.
When you see an idea you disagree with, you
can get angry, or you can learn.

ARNOLD SCHWARZENEGGER,
actor, bodybuilder and former
Governor General of California

I mentioned in the previous chapter that when you become an ally for children it is highly likely that you will find yourself on the receiving end of ridicule, anger, *ad hominem* attacks and groupthink pile-ons if you voice your opinions on social media. Sadly, there is no way to avoid these if you are set on trying to raise awareness and bring about a shift in public perception. What you can do, however, is prepare yourself for the most common criticisms and misunderstandings – forewarned is forearmed. Just remember to focus on empathy, explanation, reason and mind-mindedness when you reply. And finally, before you jump in, a good phrase I like to remember is 'not my circus, not my monkeys' – in other words, you don't have to get involved in every disagreement you come across. Sometimes keeping out of them is far better for your mental health and, ultimately, for the cause, if it means you avoid burnout.

Common myths, misconceptions and rebukes

I'd like to devote the entirety of this final chapter to the top myths, misconceptions and frequent rebukes I hear when I discuss childism, accompanied by an explanation of why and how they are flawed. I hope you find this helpful when you, inevitably, find yourself on the receiving end of them.

'Children need to toughen up; the world is a harsh place'

Let's throw this one out there first, because it's the one you're most likely to come across.

The argument is that children need to learn to deal with adversity from an early age, so they are prepared to handle the tough world they will live in when they are adults, the presumption here being that children are incapable of dealing with rejection or hardship. Often, the words 'snowflake' and 'mollycoddle' will be included somewhere in the argument. The 'kids of today' are perceived to struggle with resilience and motivation when faced with challenges or adversity, and this is blamed on supposedly overly loving and protective parents.

My answer here always starts with asking: 'But what if we create a kinder world for our children? Why do we have to accept the harshness of society today as a certainty?' This idea is a challenge to those who are childist because it invokes a lot of cognitive dissonance. The world today is harsh for them, just as it was when they were children; they didn't have anybody to support them then and, likely because of unconscious conditioning from their childhoods, they have unsupportive relationships now as adults.

It's such a simple idea, but it is an enormous concept for those who were victims of extreme childism as children to understand and accept.

The next point to consider when answering this point is the idea that neuroscience shows us that nurturing children, responding to their needs and ensuring they feel loved and supported has a significant impact on their developing brains. We know from research that children who experience more nurturing upbringings have more development in the area of the brain responsible for self-regulation. Children with good self-regulation skills are ones who will thrive the most in challenging situations as they grow and become independent. If we want to prepare children for the difficulties of the adult world (and for whatever reason we cannot, or do not, do anything to change it), then the best thing we can do is to equip them with the psychological skills necessary for them to cope with adversity. These skills will be negatively impacted if children are treated harshly – they are the children impacted the most by childism and the ones who will struggle the most with the realities of adult life.

'Children need to be more resilient'

This usually quickly follows from the previous point, commonly when discussion turns to children being allowed to quit after-school activities, clubs and the like. There is often a yearly debate, in June or July, centring on the changes that are increasingly seen in the arrangements of school sports days. Many schools now are moving towards giving participation certificates, rather than winners' medals, and class awards rather than individual winners. The argument here is that it is more inclusive of all abilities and encourages future participation in sports, which are admirable goals. Yet, each year you will find news articles and discussions on TV panel shows commenting on how silly the idea is. Usually, a commentator will say something like, 'It's ridiculous! In my day, you only got something if you won. Children today need to stop being cry-babies and be more resilient!'

What is clearly happening here is that the commentator is unconsciously remembering the childism they faced growing up. They are telling us about the times when they felt sad and were not supported in those feelings by their parents or carers. They were told to 'suck it up' – and they did, along with many other feelings that they also repressed. Did it make them more resilient? Perhaps. Or perhaps they knew that they had to get on with things that made them feel bad because there was no alternative – nobody listened to their pleas for help.

Instead of putting children through this emotional repression, we can help them to become more resilient by listening to them and helping them to work through their emotions. We can give them self-confidence by first showing them that we believe in them. We can gently encourage, coach and show children that they are capable of so much more than they think they are. And through these supportive efforts, we can teach children to develop a growth mindset, one where they have self-belief and far more genuine resilience than children who were raised to never speak out about their feelings.

'This is all some liberal, woke, lefty agenda'

A classic *ad hominem* attack, but aimed at a group, not an individual. If you hear this one, the chances are that the person saying it cannot formulate a reasoned argument to disagree with you. This indicates either that your argument is sound and they cannot find any flaws or that they don't really understand what you are talking about.

For the past decade, I have heard comments on gentle parenting, read articles, watched videos and TV segments, all mocking the parenting style. The problem is that none of them was actually talking about gentle parenting. They were all talking about permissive parenting, with no boundaries, and alternative lifestyle choices that have nothing to do with gentle parenting. Here, the best answer is to quietly educate, to fill in the missing gaps and correct the misconceptions. Ironically, many of the critics of gentle parenting were often practising the parenting style themselves; they just didn't realise it due to the myths quickly spread by the media.

With respect to liberalism – so long as it's not neoliberalism, that's a good thing. Who wouldn't argue for freedom of expression and human rights? Woke? If that means being awake to the discrimination faced by children in society today, then count me in. Lefty? A basic belief that child rights are human rights should be held by all political parties; personal choice beyond that belief is just that. Finally, if there is an agenda to usher in a more inclusive, kinder world, then that sounds pretty good to me. Of course, there isn't – yet. But watch this space!

'Gentle parenting is like a weird new cult'

I can understand that messages about kinder, gentler, more respectful and more inclusive parenting might appear to have sprung out of nowhere. After all, parenting advice has sat in the domain of the historical childcare experts for over a century now. And despite research showing authoritative parenting to be the most effective and the least damaging form, authoritarian methods still seem to be in the majority. The truth is, however, that this is not new – people have been instinctively parenting in a nurturing way for ever. They were there before the era of the historical childcare experts, they were there during it and they are still here now. These people may never have heard of the terms 'gentle parenting' or 'authoritative parenting' – that's just what they did. Because it felt right.

I have been working hard at spreading the word about gentle parenting for a decade now. It doesn't feel as if it's suddenly exploded from nowhere to me. Many others have been doing the same. Is it weird? I guess to some, especially those who grew up with the worst childism, it seems an alien concept to treat children with respect. But I think that says more about them than the parenting style. And is it a cult? Now that's just silly and not even deserving of a response.

'Parents today are all pushovers; there's no discipline!'

Oh dear, where do we start with this one? This is usually uttered by those who were on the receiving end of authoritarian discipline as children. It's likely that they were hit by their parents or carers, yelled at, shamed, punished and experienced a heavy dose of love withdrawal. To these people, discipline means hurt. It means either physical or emotional pain to deter the child from repeating the behaviour. Hello, John Watson and Little Albert (see page 34). These people need our empathy and understanding because they were almost certainly victims of childism, and it will have done them harm, despite frequent comments of 'I deserved it; I was awful.' I wish I could go back in time and meet their child selves and say, 'You don't deserve it. You deserve to be nurtured and protected. It isn't your fault; none of it is your fault. I'm sorry you are being treated this way.'

Alas, comments like 'parents today are all pushovers' usually serve to rile and anger, rather than pacify. Instead, a quick explanation of what discipline really is can help. I talk about the root of the word discipline: the Latin *'disciplina'*, which means instructions and training. I ask them who their favourite teachers were when they were at school and ask what it was about those teachers that encouraged their learning. They speak of humour, patience, humility, good listening skills, good communication and support. I ask them if they learned better from teachers with these skills than with those who yelled, punished, shamed and demanded obedience. They almost always answer 'yes'. I then ask, 'So, why do you believe children learn best from the latter? To be effective, discipline should surely embody the practices of those great teachers?' Discipline, at its heart, means keeping everybody safe and teaching children more appropriate ways to behave. There is no need for harshness. Children, just like adults, learn best when they feel good.

'Children should respect adults'

I agree. And adults should respect children. But what is implied here is that children should blindly obey adults. They should not question them; they should do what they're told, when they're told. They should acquiesce, regardless of how the treatment makes them feel. 'Children should respect adults' is rooted in childism. It is upheld by those who were forced to deny their emotions as children, in order to appease adults.

Children should respect everybody; so should adults. It should be a default setting in society. Sadly, those who demand respect from children are often the least respectful people. The reality is that if adults behave in disrespectful ways, then they lose any respect, not just from children, but from other adults, too. What they end up with is a fear-based response. People do what they ask because they are scared of the repercussions if they don't. That is not respect. It is important to point out that true respect is mutual, and if there is no reciprocation from the adult, then the child is simply obeying because of fear.

'Mollycoddling children does them no good – it makes them soft'

This is often tied to comments about sleep training or tackling tantrums. Sometimes it is related to separation anxiety and starting daycare. Whatever the scenario, the underlying idea is that comforting crying and upset children somehow does them more harm than good. Instead, the belief is that children should repress their emotions and become independent from their primary attachment figures as early as possible.

Often, those who state opinions like this have trauma in their backgrounds. You may well find loss, premature separation from parents (for instance, being sent to boarding school) or emotionally unavailable parents in their histories. Sadly, they grew without the love and comfort they needed to thrive, learning they could only rely on themselves and now holding the mistaken belief that it is good for children to go through the same as they did, to toughen them up. This view prevents them from considering that what they experienced as children was damaging; it is a self-protection mechanism and, sadly, it also means they perpetuate the detached style of child raising for future generations. The response here is simply one of empathy, rather than try to change their mind.

'This is all political correctness gone mad'

I'm not sure what political correctness means in this sense. Does it mean considering human rights? Does it mean reducing discrimination? Improving equity? Does it mean the reduction of racism, sexism, ableism and the discrimination of those who identify as LGBTQ+? Alas, politics aren't big on reducing discrimination. Far from it. And is it the right thing to do? Yes, I believe it is. I believe we all have a duty to be kinder. So I guess the word 'correct' is right.

Often, the people who use this phrase are indicating that they are uncomfortable with the speed of social change. Everything seems to be constantly shifting; technology, societal demographics and scientific understanding to name a few. This can leave those from older generations, firm in the beliefs with which they were raised, feeling lost at sea; they are anchorless, drifting away from the security of their racist, homophobic, sexist, childist homeland in new, uncharted waters, and they feel insecure. Rather than embracing change for the better, they cling to the old discrimination they were raised with and, instead, attack the change and those who are trying to instigate it. This comment isn't about you, or me or anybody else who is passionate about social activism. It is about them and their discomfort with the changing world. The response here again is predominantly one of empathy and understanding what the person has gone through to leave them feeling this way. You won't change their mind so it is better to preserve your peace by ending the conversation as quickly as possible.

'We do so much for our children already. They're spoiled!'

This is true. Parenting is relentless. Children have constant needs twenty-four hours of every day. There is no holiday. There are no sabbaticals. There is little help. Children devour our incomes, time and emotional reserves. It seems like they have everything they need and more. The trouble is, we can't make up for childism with gifts and activities. Preparing gourmet meals with home-grown organic vegetables does not negate childism. Purchasing hundreds of pounds' worth of birthday gifts does not negate childism. Expensive holidays and day trips do not negate childism. And a wardrobe full of clothes and a toy box full of toys do not negate childism.

Children may be 'spoiled' with belongings, gifts and activities, yet still yearn for love and acceptance. They can have the most privileged of upbringings financially, yet go through life never having their needs for connection, understanding and support fulfilled. To add to this, you cannot spoil a child with love. It is impossible to nurture them too much. Sadly, it is commonly those who didn't feel loved enough (but often don't realise) who are the loudest critics of so-called spoiling children with love.

'It's for their own good. They can't grow up learning that it's OK to deliberately misbehave and manipulate people!'

This comment highlights a huge misunderstanding of child development, and is commonly made by those who believe that toddlers tantrum deliberately to control adults and to manipulate them into doing or giving them what they want. Of course, we know this is incorrect. Neurologically speaking, toddlers (and children of any age, even teens – because tantrums are by no means unique to toddlerhood) tantrum because they are lacking in emotion-regulation skills and impulse control. This is normal for their age. The areas of the brain responsible for these skills are not fully developed until an individual is in their twenties (years, not months). Of course, toddlers (and other ages) are dysregulated and struggle to control their emotions when they are triggered. They *cannot* behave in other ways; they cannot calm down if they lack the necessary brain development.

In fact, when children are so dysregulated that they are screaming and sobbing, they probably feel far worse than the surrounding adults. Can you imagine feeling that out of control and being unable to stop yourself? Here, the adults are the only ones with the ability to self-regulate and calm down. When they display the sort of calm behaviour they hope to see in their children, they help them to be calmer and, ultimately, this is what teaches children self-regulation skills. If, however, they ignore the child's distress in the mistaken belief that if they do respond they will somehow be reinforcing the behaviour (hello again, John Watson!), then the child has only one option: to repress their emotions in the quest to be loved and accepted by their parent or carer again. But what happens to these repressed emotions? In time, they can become internalising behaviours, with the hurtful feelings driven inwards, resulting in anxiety, depression and trust issues in relationships. Leaving a child in a dysregulated state is never for their own good.

'It's important for babies to learn to self-soothe'

If we could change one word in this sentence, I would agree with it. Swapping the word 'important' for the word 'impossible', it makes much more sense!

Quite simply, babies cannot self-soothe. The implication of the word 'soothe' here is that something is wrong in their world. Perhaps they are too hot or too cold? Perhaps they are in pain? Perhaps the room is too dark or too light? Perhaps they are hungry or thirsty? To suggest that a baby can self-soothe means that they are able to resolve these physical problems independently. We are presuming that they can turn the heating on or off, open or close the curtains or blinds, administer their own pain relief and go to the kitchen to prepare themselves a drink or some food. And, of course, they can't do any of these things. The only thing they can do is to indicate their distress to their carers through their tears.

Similarly, they cannot self-soothe emotional problems. If they are scared or anxious, they cannot engage in a deep-breathing exercise. If they are concerned that they have been abandoned (during a period of separation anxiety), they cannot give you a call or a text and check you're still in the next room. If they are not tired, they cannot count sheep or take a herbal sleep supplement. They only have one solution to all these problems and, once again, it is to cry for their carers or parents. In fact, you could argue that babies can self-soothe *by* crying for their parents or carers. Crying ultimately fixes all problems because they trust we can help them. What they can't do is to get into a state of physical or psychological homeostasis without us. If they could, that would be seriously impressive, because it would indicate brain development well beyond their years!

What really happens when babies are left to cry? Again, the only thing we can really teach them this way is to repress their needs. We teach them to not cry, to not disturb us at night. We know research into sleep training shows that babies who have been through a process of being sleep trained do not sleep any more – they just remain quiet when they are awake. I'm not sure that this is really what any parent wants for their children?

'It's important to scare them to stop them doing dangerous things'

Absolutely, it is important to keep children (and adults and animals) safe. Sometimes you may need to be less gentle when doing so – for instance, yelling at a child you can't physically reach who is about to run into a road. Here, safety trumps everything. As adults, it is our duty to keep children safe. Once they are safe, however, we have two options: we can apologise for any fear we caused, explain that we were scared (hence the yelling) and we can talk about road sense (or the safety issue in question); or we can continue to yell and also smack, punish, shame and scare. The latter is a childist response and, sadly, one that is most common in society today. It also teaches children little about more appropriate behaviour.

'Childism doesn't exist, it's just another made up "ism" for people to get worked up about'

If you come across this one, you can guarantee that the person saying it has read nothing about childism. You can also pretty much guarantee that they have lived a life of privilege – because they are also quietly indicating that they are fed up with hearing about racism, sexism, ableism and homophobia. Anybody who doesn't believe in 'isms' or ridicules them is really highlighting quite how much harm they came to in their own childhood. Their lack of social awareness and empathy are evidence for why it is so important to be conscious of and fight against childism. Sadly, there is no getting through to people like this because the cognitive dissonance is just too strong. In this case, preserve your wellbeing and walk away or block them.

'It never did me any harm!'

I refer you back to the entirety of Chapter 8!

The sad reality is that this comment is usually one of the biggest indicators of harm caused by childism, but the person saying it is usually unaware of this, so continues to repeat it for future generations. It's time to break the cycle of harm now.

'This is all right when you have little kids – but try parenting teenagers!'

The beauty of anti-childist parenting is that you reap the rewards of all your hard work when your children grow. If children are raised with respect and a focus on connection, this remains a central part of the parent–child relationship over time. Parenting teens who have been raised using gentle, respectful, anti-childist measures is a joy. Of course, you have to be aware of child development – the teen brain is hugely different from that of a fully grown adult and their behaviour can be infuriating and confusing as a result. However, if you are close to your teen, then you trust each other, you communicate well and you love and respect each other, and you will make it through the teen years relatively unscathed and with a beautiful relationship with your almost-adult child at the end of them.

If a young child is raised using harsh, authoritarian parenting, relying on creating fear through threats of punishments or controlling through the dangling of rewards, then you are going to struggle in the teen years. When children are bigger than you, you cannot intimidate them or drag them to the naughty step. Teens are not easily bribed by stickers and sweets either. At this point, authoritarian parents find themselves coming unstuck because what they have relied on for many years no longer works. In short, the more childist the early years, the more troublesome the teen years will be.

'It's OK when you've only got one child, but it's impossible when you have two or more.'

Caring for a group of children is hard, whether you're a parent or professional childcare worker. And no matter how you raise your children it's going to be hard work. If you're outnumbered you will have frustrating, exhausting days. This is unavoidable, whatever your beliefs on childism. Sadly, we lack the social support we so desperately need to raise children; and this is the fault of our neoliberalist governments. All parents need more financial, emotional and practical support.

'I've seen the results of this so-called gentle parenting, and it doesn't work – it raises brats'

Parenting is a long game. Child development means that you cannot speed a child's brain growth and connectivity. Babies are still going to wake up at night. Toddlers are still going to tantrum. Siblings are still going to fight. Teenagers are still going to refuse to get up in the morning and struggle to communicate their feelings rationally. All these behaviours are normal for these ages. No matter how you choose to discipline your children, the results cannot be measured fully until they become adults – because, ultimately, you're raising them with a view to the future adult they will become. There are no magic quick fixes that stop children behaving like children.

Children who have been raised with a more authoritarian parenting style will often appear to be better behaved, especially when they are younger. However, this is not because they are making better moral decisions; it is simply that they are scared to express their emotions. They are frozen in fear and fawning as defence mechanisms. They have learned that obedience and compliance result in better treatment from their parents. And while these quiet and compliant children may seem like the 'perfect' children when they are younger, the chances of the parent–child relationship fracturing during the teen years is extremely high, as are mental-health repercussions in adulthood.

'Parenting trends come and go; future generations will laugh at this'

Maybe. Although if we strip everything back and focus on respect and kindness, treating children's rights as human rights, I don't see how this is laughable.

I suspect that what will actually happen in the future is that the research into the neurological and emotional impacts of parenting styles will become more sophisticated, and authoritative parenting will have even more of an impressive evidence base. I suspect that we will look back in horror at the thought of hitting or scaring children in the name of discipline. If I'm wrong, that's OK too, because I don't think that too much kindness is ever a bad thing, and if people laugh at me for that, then so be it.

'This just sounds like it's shaming and guilting parents'

No! Quite the opposite. Being an anti-childist ally means being aware of the childism we all faced in our own childhoods. It means showing empathy to those who are struggling with the idea and who are carrying too much pain and repressed emotion to be able to tackle their inherited beliefs. At its core, being anti-childist means supporting all parents, letting them see the obstacles that sit in the way of easier parenting, helping them to learn that their emotional outbursts are not their fault and allowing them to feel some peace about the relationship they had with their own parents. This work is not about shame or guilt. It is the very opposite; it is about forgiveness and understanding.

'It's impossible to be a perfect parent. I live in the real world'

I absolutely agree! There's no such thing as a perfect parent and aiming to be one is highly damaging. It's important for parents to mess up sometimes, so long as they apologise and make things right afterwards. It is these moments of rupture and repair (or as I call them holler and heal) that teach children how to resolve tricky situations in the future. These moments are also important because they teach our children that nobody is perfect – even their parents. This helps them to feel happier with their own mistakes and improves resilience as they grow – because they learn from us that you can always correct, or make amends for, mistakes you make. Parenting today is tough, however you choose to raise your children. We tend to place far too much pressure on ourselves and feel overly guilty when we slip up. The thing is, those mistakes show that we're trying – and, ultimately, they help us to learn, too. Sometimes we learn how to do something so that our children respond better; sometimes that learning is about ourselves.

The transition to becoming a parent tends to open old wounds and lay bare any issues in our relationships, so not only do we have to learn how to keep a tiny new human alive and safe, we also have to revisit hurtful experiences from our pasts and learn how to navigate changing relationships and differing beliefs in the present, too. Nobody can possibly get through this amount of physical and psychological work and not lose it at times.

I am a great fan of the work of the British paediatrician and psychoanalyst Donald Winnicott, who advocated for 'good enough' parenting. This approach allows parents to aim to be their best, but not beat themselves up too much when they come up short of their goals. Personally, I try to be the best gentle, respectful parent I can be 70 per cent of the time and allow myself the grace to fail the remaining 30 per cent. So long as you keep trying and you're 'good enough', that really is all that matters.

Becoming an anti-childist ally means understanding all the baggage we bring with us to parenting and how that impacts us; it shows parents empathy as well as children. It also calls out governments who have made parenting today such a difficult job, for so many reasons. In short, being anti-childist is the antithesis of perfect parenting and the unrealistic messages and advice spread by the historical childcare experts over the last century.

'The young people of today are rude, antisocial and poorly behaved'

Actually, today's children, including teenagers, are some of the best behaved ever. They smoke and drink less and exhibit less antisocial behaviour. They also show higher levels of empathy and prosocial behaviour.[1] If this is due to a rise in gentle and respectful parenting, imagine how great they would be if we could eradicate childism entirely?

It's easy to view our own childhoods through rose-tinted spectacles. But often we forget the antisocial behaviour and harmful activities our friends, classmates and maybe even we ourselves took part in. The trend for older generations to blame 'the youth of today' for being out of control is not new. If we could trace back reports a hundred years or more, there would still be statements blaming 'the youth of today' for all the ills in society.

'Why do young people today get so offended at everything?'

I'm not sure they do. The difference is they are finally feeling more able to express their views. Children have the right to hold their own beliefs and freedom to express them. Despite this, historically their voices have been repressed. In the past, children learned that their opinions were worth less than those of an adult. They learned to be quiet and to not question adult authority. Being anti-childist means giving children a voice and listening to them. They are the future of this world, and what they have to say is important.

'Children need to obey their elders!'

Why? I understand concerns of safety, and sometimes children really do need to trust adults to keep them safe. But outside of this, why do they need to blindly obey? If adults do not have good reasons for their instructions, what they are asking is not informed by a good understanding of child development and their requests are childist, therefore why should children obey them? Very often, adults tend to repeat cycles of behaviour that they learned from their own parents.

One of the reasons I called this book *Because I Said So!* is because this is the phrase that was used in my own family. As a child, I learned that I wasn't allowed to question adults – because they said so. I would ask 'Why?' but sensible reasoning rarely followed, just a repeat of 'Because I said so'. It is the most irrational phrase, as is the idea of children needing to obey adults. We need to learn to effectively communicate with children and to explain our reasoning to them. Sadly, many adults cannot do this because they quickly realise how unreasonable their requests are.

I hope that you will not find yourself on the receiving end of these statements often; I know how stressful and draining it can feel, working on your own self-regulation and staying calm and collected when inside you feel like screaming.

That said, there is a part of me that actually hopes you *do* hear these statements, and gently respond to them, often. If this happens, it will mean that more and more people are starting to talk about childism and question the reasons and beliefs that underpin the discrimination of children in our society today. It also means that you are playing a key role in, hopefully, creating a better world for future generations.

A Closing Note

Thank you for coming on this journey with me, even though I am sure at times it has been an uncomfortable one.

When I was writing this book, I often veered between feeling excited and fired up to usher in positive social change and deeply despondent and depressed at the state of the world I have brought my children into. I think we have to take such feelings of anger, sadness and frustration and bottle them – not to repress them (because I hope by this point you know how damaging that is), but to use them as fuel to move forwards when we run into the inevitable naysayers and childism deniers. By taking ourselves back to a place where we can utilise our exasperation and despair as a force for good, a force for change, we can absolutely make a difference.

We don't only owe this fight for change to our children and future generations. We owe it to our parents, grandparents and the ancestors who came before them, all of whom suffered at the hands of childism. We also owe it to ourselves to recognise the childism we experienced as children, to stop dismissing poor treatment as something we deserved. Our quest to change the world for the better for our children gives us an amazing opportunity to heal ourselves. The power of realising that we have always been worthy of love and respect (even on the days we believed ourselves to be most unlovable) can be transformative. In being kinder towards the children in our lives today, we are also offered an opportunity to be kind to the inner child that lives within us. Far from fracturing relationships, this can help us to heal generational pain – to forgive and to truly understand the actions of our parents and carers. Becoming anti-childist has the potential to change the world for everyone. But one thing is for certain: it will definitely change yours – if you let it.

We are all responsible for calling out childism. We are all members of society, and we all have the power to make change. Some may call us snowflakes, but do you know what is so astounding about snowflakes? An individual one is not going to dramatically change a landscape. When many snowflakes fall together, however – when they become a blizzard – each of them joins with others, blanketing the landscape, changing it into something entirely different. If individually we are snowflakes, then as a community, we can be the blizzard. We can be the ones who change the landscape of childism. We need to turn cries of 'because I said so' into calls of 'because child rights are human rights'. Our voices, like snowflakes, are stronger when they are together.

I'd like to leave the very last words of this book, to one of the most famous and most loved social activists of all time, Nelson Mandela:

There can be no keener revelation of a society's soul than the way in which it treats its children.

Further Reading and Resources

Sarah's social media

Sarah's Facebook: www.facebook.com/
  sarahockwellsmithauthor
Sarah's Instagram: www.instagram.com/sarahockwellsmith
Sarah's TikTok: www.tiktok.com/sarahockwellsmith
Sarah's Twitter: www.twitter.com/thebabyexpert
Sarah's website: www.sarahockwell-smith.com
Sarah's anti-childist Facebook discussion group:
  www.facebook.com/groups/becauseisaidso

Sarah's other books that touch on childism

*How to be a Calm Parent: Lose the guilt, control your anger and
  tame the stress – for more peaceful and enjoyable parenting and
  calmer, happier children too* (Piatkus, 2022)
*The Gentle Parenting Book: How to raise calmer, happier children
  from birth to seven: updated and revised* (Piatkus, 2023)
*The Gentle Discipline Book: How to raise co-operative, polite and
  helpful children* (Piatkus, 2016)
The Gentle Sleep Book (Piatkus 2020)

Recommended websites

Save the Children, www.savethechildren.org.uk
Action for Children, www.actionforchildren.org.uk
YoungMinds, www.youngminds.org.uk
Lives in the Balance, www.livesinthebalance.org
Children in Scotland, www.childreninscotland.org.uk
The Children's Society, www.childrenssociety.org.uk
National Children's Bureau, www.ncb.org.uk
British Youth Council, www.byc.org.uk
Children and Young People's Mental Health Coalition,
     www.cypmhc.org.uk
IPSEA (SEND rights advice), www.ipsea.org.uk
Just for Kids Law, www.justforkidslaw.org
Youth Justice Legal Centre, www.yjlc.uk
CRAE (Children's Rights Alliance for England), www.crae.org.uk
The Childism Institute, www.childism.org

Further reading about childism

Young-Bruehl, E., *Childism: Confronting Prejudice Against Children*
     (Yale University Press, 2012)

Further reading about neoliberalism for early-years workers

Roberts-Holmes, G. and Moss, P., *Neoliberalism and Early
     Childhood Education: Markets, Imaginaries and Governance*
     (Routledge, 2021)

References

Chapter 1

1. Pierce, C., Allen, G., 1975, 'Childism', published in *Psychiatric Annals*, 2013;5(7):15–24.
2. Young-Bruehl, E., *Childism: Confronting Prejudice Against Children* (Yale University Press, 2012)
3. The Universal Declaration of Human Rights: www.un.org/sites/un2.un.org/files/2021/03/udhr.pdf
4. 'Declaration of the Rights of the Child – 1923', Child Rights International Network, https://archive.crin.org/en/library/un-regional-documentation/declaration-rights-child-1923
5. The United Nations Convention on the Rights of the Child ©OHCHR 1996–2023 www.ohchr.org/en/instruments-mechanisms/instruments/convention-rights-child
6. Physical punishment and discipline of children: how the law is changing, Scottish government factsheet www.gov.scot/publications/physical-punishment-and-discipline-of-children-how-the-law-is-changing/
7. Ending physical punishment in Wales: www.gov.wales/ending-physical-punishment-children
8. Children Act 2004: www.legislation.gov.uk/ukpga/2004/31/section/
9. Be Reasonable, Scotland: www.bereasonablescotland.org/
10. The *Guardian*, 2022, 'England should follow Scotland and Wales and ban smacking says children's tsar': www.theguardian.com/society/2022/apr/21/england-should-follow-scotland-and-wales-and-ban-smacking-says-childrens-tsar
11. YouGov report, 2021, 'Smacking: Parents who were physically punished as children are more likely to punish their children'.

https://yougov.co.uk/topics/society/articles-reports/2021/09/27/
smacking-parents-who-were-physically-punished-child

12. Gillick v. West Norfolk and Wisbech Area Health Authority
(1985) 2 A11 ER 402.

Chapter 2

1. https://www.elle.com/beauty/makeup-skin-care/news/a43899/
cate-blanchett-skii-beauty-interview/
2. Watson, J. B., 1928, 'The Psychological Care of Infant and Child'.
3. Emmett Holt, L, E., 1894, 'The Care and Feeding of Children'.
4. Green, C., 1984, *Toddler Taming*, Ebury Press.
5. Ferber, R., 1985, *Solve Your Child's Sleep Problems*, Dorling
Kindersley.
6. Truby King, F., 1913, *Feeding and care of baby'*, issued by the Royal
New Zealand Society for the Health of Women & Children.
7. Plunket – www.plunket.org.nz
8. Pearl, M. and Pearl, D., 1994, *To Train up a Child*, No Greater Joy
Ministries; 'Child "training" book triggers backlash', BBC website:
www.bbc.co.uk/news/magazine-25268343
9. Watson, J. B., 1928, 'The Psychological Care of Infant and Child'.

Chapter 3

1. Price, A. M., Wake, M., Ukoumunne O. C., et al., 2012, 'Five-
year follow-up of harms and benefits of behavioral infant sleep
intervention: Randomized trial', *Pediatrics*, 130(4):643–51.
2. Hall, W. A., Hutton, E., Brant, R. F., et al. 2015, 'A randomized
controlled trial of an intervention for infants' behavioral sleep
problems'. *BMC Pediatrics*, 2015 Nov 13;15:181.

Chapter 4

1. Li Yuanyuan J. and Liu Yuanyuan (2018), 'Are Parents Patient?
The Influence of Parenting Role Salience and Parental Status on
Impatience,' *Frontiers in Psychology*, Vol. 9: 1523.
2. Regalado, M., Sareen, H., Inkelas, M., Wissow, L. S. and Halfon,
N., 2004, 'Parents' discipline of young children: results from the
National Survey of Early Childhood Health'. *Pediatrics*. Jun;113(6
Suppl):1952–8.
3. Ibid.
4. Ibid.

5. Frost, J., 2011, *Confident Toddler Care: The Ultimate Guide to The Toddler Years*, Orion (1st edition).

6. NHS website, 'Temper Tantrums' – www.nhs.uk/conditions/baby/babys-development/behaviour/temper-tantrums/

7. Smith, K. (2010) 'Parenting', in Hansen, K., Jones, E., Joshni, H. and Budge, D. (editors) 'Millennium Cohort Study Fourth Survey: A User's Guide to Initial Findings', London: Institute of Education University of London.

8. Ibid.

9. YouGov report, 2021, 'Smacking: Parents who were physically punished as children are more likely to punish their children'. https://yougov.co.uk/topics/society/articles-reports/2021/09/27/smacking-parents-who-were-physically-punished-chil

10. Mathews, B., Pacella, R., Dunne, M., Scott, J. et al. 2021, 'The Australian Child Maltreatment Study (ACMS): protocol for a national survey of the prevalence of child abuse and neglect, associated mental disorders and physical health problems, and burden of disease', *BMJ Open*, May 11;11(5).

11. Finkelhorn, E., Turner, H., et al. 2019, 'Corporal Punishment: Current Rates from a National Survey', *Journal of Child and Family Studies*. 28, pages 1991–7.

12. American Academy of Pediatrics Policy Statement, 2018, 'Effective Discipline to Raise Healthy Children', *Pediatrics*, Vol. 142, Issue 6.

13. Taylor, C. A., Fleckman, J. M., Scholer, S. J. and Branco, N., 2018, 'US Pediatricians' Attitudes, Beliefs, and Perceived Injunctive Norms About Spanking', *Journal of Developmental and Behavioural Pediatrics*, Sep;39(7):564–72.

14. Gershoff, E. T. and Grogan-Kaylor, A., 2016, 'Spanking and child outcomes: Old controversies and new meta-analyses'. *Journal of Family Psychology*. Jun;30(4):453–69.

15. Tom Bennett Independent Review of Behaviour in Schools: https://assets.publishing.service.gov.uk/government/uploads/system/uploads/attachment_data/file/602487/Tom_Bennett_Independent_Review_of_Behaviour_in_Schools.pdf

16. Tom Bennet Twitter: https://twitter.com/tombennett71/status/1062111476381638656

17. Sealy, J., Abrams, E. and Cockburn, T., 2020, 'Students' experience of isolation room punishment in UK mainstream education. "I can't put into words what you felt like, almost a dog in a cage"', *International Journal of Inclusive Education*.

18. Atkinson, M., 2013. Always Someone Else's Problem: Office of the

Children's Commissioner's Report on Illegal Exclusions. London: Office of the Children's Commissioner.

19. Ibid.

Chapter 5

1. Chomsky, N,. 1998, *Profit over people: Neoliberalism and the Global Order*, Seven Stories Press, US.

2. Education secretary speech 2021 on MATS: www.gov.uk/government/speeches/education-secretary-speech-to-the-confederation-of-school-trusts

3. Multi Academy Trusts report: https://lordslibrary.parliament.uk/education-multi-academy-trusts/

4. Sims, M. (2017), 'Neoliberalism and early childhood'. *Cogent Education*, 4(1): Article 1365411.

5. O'Regan, F. (2009), 'Persistent disruptive behaviour and exclusion'. *ADHD in Practice*, 1(1): 8–11

6. https://www.huffpost.com/entry/sheryl-sandberg-is-half-r_b_2871382

7. LaingBuisson UK Market Report 16ed, 2021, accessed online: www.laingbuisson.com/shop/childcare-uk-market-report-16ed/

8. National Careers Service, nursery worker profile: www.nationalcareers.service.gov.uk/job-profiles/nursery-worker

9. Main summary survey of childcare and early-years providers, 2021: https://assets.publishing.service.gov.uk/government/uploads/system/uploads/attachment_data/file/1039675/Main_summary_survey_of_childcare_and_early_years_providers_2021.pdf

10. Moss, P. and Roberts-Holmes, G. 2022. 'Now is the time! Confronting neo-liberalism in early childhood.' *Contemporary Issues in Early Childhood*, 23(1), 96–99

11. Destatis, day care statistics report: *https://www.destatis.de/EN/Themes/Society-Environment/Social-Statistics/Day-Care-Children/_node.html*

12. UNICEF, where do rich countries stand on childcare report: www.unicef-irc.org/where-do-rich-countries-stand-on-childcare

13. Children's Mental Health Week: www.childrensmentalhealthweek.org.uk/

14. Mental health of children and young people survey, 2017, https://digital.nhs.uk/data-and-information/publications/statistical/mental-health-of-children-and-young-people-in-england/2021-follow-up-to-the-2017-survey

15. Child mental health waiting times, the *Independent* online: www. independent.co.uk/news/health/child-mental-health-waiting-times-b1972830.html

16. O'Dowd, A., 2021, 'Sure Start children's centres prevented 13 000 hospital admissions a year, study estimates', *BMJ*, 374

17. Ibid.

18. DfE, 2023, Press Release: https://www.gov.uk/government/news/ thousands-of-families-to-benefit-from-local-support-in-rollout-of-family-hubs

19. Action for children, 'Where is child poverty increasing in the UK?' report: www.actionforchildren.org.uk/blog/ where-is-child-poverty-increasing-in-the-uk/

20. USA Census, 2022, Poverty rates by age group report: https:// www.census.gov/library/stories/2022/10/poverty-rate-varies-by-age-groups.html

21. Shelter, '1 in every 100 children in England will wake up homeless this Christmas' press release: https://england. shelter.org.uk/media/press_release/1_in_every_100_children_ in_england_will_wake_up_homeless_this_christmas; The Trussell Trust, end-of-year stats report: www.trusselltrust.org/ news-and-blog/latest-stats/end-year-stats/

22. Pinderhughes, E. E., Dodge, K. A., Bates, J. E., et al. 2000, 'Discipline responses: influences of parents' socioeconomic status, ethnicity, beliefs about parenting, stress, and cognitive-emotional processes', *Journal of Family Psychology*, 14(3), 380–400.

Chapter 6

1. Microsoft digital civility report, 2019. https://blogs.microsoft. com/on-the-issues/2019/10/09/teens-say-parents-share-too-much-about-them-online-microsoft-study/

2. Moser, C., Chen, T., et al., 2017, 'Parents' and Children's Preferences about Parents Sharing about Children on Social Media', *Proceedings of the 2017 CHI Conference on Human Factors in Computing Systems*, May, 5221–5.

3. Ibid.

4. Amon, M, J., et al., 2022, 'Sharenting and Children's Privacy in the United States: Parenting Style, Practices, and Perspectives on Sharing Young Children's Photos on Social Media', in *Proceedings of the ACM on Human-Computer Interaction*, Vol. 6, CSCW1, Article 116.

5. Brosch, A., 2016, 'When the Child is Born into the Internet: Sharenting as a Growing Trend among Parents on Facebook', *New Educational Review*, 43(1):225–35.

6. The *Independent*, 'Teenager sues over embarrassing childhood pictures on Facebook': www.independent.co.uk/news/world/ europe/teenager-sues-parents-over-embarrassing-childhood-pictures-on-facebook-austria-a7307561.html

7. GDPR https://ico.org.uk/for-organisations/guide-to-data-protection/guide-to-the-general-data-protection-regulation-gdpr/ children-and-the-uk-gdpr/what-should-our-general-approach-to-processing-children-s-personal-data-be/

8. BKA Press Release: www.bka.de/DE/Presse/Listenseite_ Pressemitteilungen/2021/Presse2021/210503_pmboystown.html

9. *Wired*, 2014, '80 percent dark web visits relate to pedophilia': www.wired.com/2014/12/80-percent-dark-web-visits-relate-pedophilia-study-finds/

10. Basu, K., Hussain, S., Gupta, U., 2020 'COPPTCHA: COPPA Tracking by Checking Hardware-Level Activity', *IEEE Transactions on Information Forensics and Security*, 2020; 15: 3213

Chapter 7

1. Hoffman, M. L. and Saltzstein, H. D. (1967). 'Parent discipline and the child's moral development', *Journal of Personality and Social Psychology*, 5(1), 45–57.

2. Choe, D. E., Olson, S. L., Sameroff, A. J., 2013, 'The interplay of externalizing problems and physical and inductive discipline during childhood', *Developmental Psychology*. 2029–39.

3. Chang, H., Olson, S. L., Sameroff, A. J., et al., 2010, 'Child Effortful Control as a Mediator of Parenting Practices on Externalizing Behavior: Evidence for a Sex-Differentiated Pathway across the Transition from Preschool to School', *Journal of Abnormal Child Psychology*, July:71–81.

4. Krevans, J. and Gibbs, J. C., 1996, 'Parents' Use of Inductive Discipline: Relations to Children's Empathy and Prosocial Behavior', *Child Development*, December 1996:3263.

5. Csapo B., 1997, 'The Development of Inductive Reasoning: Cross-sectional Assessments in an Educational Context', *International Journal of Behavioral Development*, 20(4):609–26.

6. Eisenberg, N. and Morris, A. S., 2001, Social Justice Research. 95–120.

7. Benchaya, M. C., Bisch, N. K., Moreira, T. C., et al., 2011.

'Non-authoritative parents and impact on drug use: the perception of adolescent children', *Journal of Pediatrics*. 87(3):238–44.

8. Yamagata, S., Takahashi, Y., Ozaki, K., et al., 2013, 'Bidirectional influences between maternal parenting and children's peer problems: a longitudinal monozygotic twin difference study.' *Developmental Science*, 16(2):249–59.

9. Piko, B. F.and Balázs, M. Á., 2012, 'Authoritative parenting style and adolescent smoking and drinking', *Addictive Behavior*, Mar;37(3):353–6.

10. Kiefner-Burmeister, A. and Hinman, N., 2020, 'The Role of General Parenting Style in Child Diet and Obesity Risk', *Current Nutrition Reports*, Mar;9(1):14–30.

11. Cong, E. Z., Cai, Y. Y., Wang, Y., et al., 2021, 'Association of depression and suicidal ideation with parenting style in adolescents', *Zhongguo Dang Dai Er Ke Za Zhi*. Sept 15;23(9):938–43.

12. Eun, J. D., Paksarian, D., He, J. P., et al., 2018, 'Parenting style and mental disorders in a nationally representative sample of US adolescents', *Social Psychiatry and Psychiatric Epidemiology*. Jan; 53(1):11–20.

13. Maté, G., 2018, *In the Realm of Hungry Ghosts: Close Encounters with Addiction*, Vermilion.

14. Philbrook, L. E., Hozella, A. C., Kim, B. R., et al., 2014, 'Maternal emotional availability at bedtime and infant cortisol at 1 and 3 months', *Early Human Development*, Oct;90(10):595–605.

15. Beijers, R., Riksen-Walraven, J. M. and De Weerth, C., 2013, 'Cortisol regulation in 12-month-old human infants: associations with the infants' early history of breastfeeding and co-sleeping', *Stress*. May;16(3):267–77.

16. Luby, J. L., Barch, D. M., Belden, A., et al., 2012, 'Maternal support in early childhood predicts larger hippocampal volumes at school age', *Proceedings of the National Academy of Sciences U S A*, Feb 21;109(8):2854–9.

17. Bélanger, M.-È., Bernier, A., Simard, V., et al., 2015, 'Attachment and sleep among toddlers: disentangling attachment security and dependency', *Monographs of the Society for Research in Child Development*, Mar;80(1):125–40.

18. Mcleod, J. D. and Shanahan, M. J., 1996, 'Trajectories of poverty and children's mental health', *Journal of Health and Social Behaviour*, Sep;37(3):207–20.

19. Dashiff, C., DiMicco, W., Myers, B., et al., 2009, 'Poverty

and adolescent mental health', *Journal of Child and Adolescent Psychiatric Nursing*, Feb;22(1):23–32.

20. Zaneva, M., Guzman-Holst, C., Reeves, A., et al., 2022, 'The Impact of Monetary Poverty Alleviation Programs on Children's and Adolescents' Mental Health: A Systematic Review and Meta-Analysis Across Low-, Middle-, and High-Income Countries', *Journal of Adolescent Health*. Aug;71(2):147–56.

21. Moe, C. A., Kovski, N .L., Dalve, K., et al., 2022, 'Cumulative Payments Through the Earned Income Tax Credit Program in Childhood and Criminal Conviction During Adolescence in the US', *JAMA Network Open*, Nov 1;5(11).

22. Troller-Renfree, S. V., Costanzo, M. A., Duncan, G. J., et al., 2022, 'The impact of a poverty reduction intervention on infant brain activity', *Proceedings of the National Academy of Science*, U S A, Feb 1;119(5).

23. Robinson, K., 2010, *The Element: How Finding Your Passion Changes Everything*, Penguin.

24. The Thrive Approach: www.thriveapproach.com/

25. Endedijk, H. M., Breeman, L. D., Van Lissa, C. J., et al., 2022. 'The Teacher's Invisible Hand: A Meta-Analysis of the Relevance of Teacher–Student Relationship Quality for Peer Relationships and the Contribution of Student Behavior.' *Review of Educational Research*, 92(3), 370–412.

26. Korpershoek, H., Harms, T., De Boer, H., et al., 2016. 'A Meta-Analysis of the Effects of Classroom Management Strategies and Classroom Management Programs on Students' Academic, Behavioral, Emotional, and Motivational Outcomes', *Review of Educational Research*, 86(3), 643–80.

27. Kasikci, F. and Ozhan, M. B., 2021, 'Prediction of Academic Achievement and Happiness in Middle School Students: The role of social-emotional learning skills', *Inquiry in Education*, volume 13, issue 2, Article 15.

28. CASEL: https://casel.org/fundamentals-of-sel/what-is-the-casel-framework

29. Jessiman, P., Kidger, J., Spencer, L., et al., 2022, 'School culture and student mental health: a qualitative study in UK secondary schools', BMC Public Health, 22, 619.

30. Moskowitz, S. and Dewaelel, J. M., 2019, 'Is teacher happiness contagious? A study of the link between perceptions of language teacher happiness and student attitudes', *Innovation in Language Learning and Teaching* 15(1).

31. Greene, R. W., 2014, *Lost at School: Why Our Kids with Behavioral*

Challenges are Falling Through the Cracks and How We Can Help Them, Scribner.

32. Grimm, F., Alcock, B., Butler, J., et al., 2022, 'Improving children and young people's mental health services: Local data insights from England, Scotland and Wales'. *The Health Foundation*.

33. Singh, S. P. and Tuomainen, H., 2015, 'Transition from child to adult mental health services: needs, barriers, experiences and new models of care', *World Psychiatry*. Oct;14(3):358–61.

Chapter 8

1. Festinger, L., 1957, *A Theory of Cognitive Dissonance,* Stanford University Press.

2. Ibid.

3. Font, S. A. and Maguire-Jack, K., 2016, 'Pathways from childhood abuse and other adversities to adult health risks: The role of adult socioeconomic conditions', *Child Abuse and Neglect,* Jan;51:390–9.

4. Gunnar, M. R. and Quevedo, K. M., 2008, 'Early care experiences and HPA axis regulation in children: a mechanism for later trauma vulnerability', *Progress in Brain Research*, 167:137–49.

5. Franklin-Luther, P. and Volk, A., 2021, 'The links between adult personality, parental discipline attitudes and harsh child punishment', *Journal of Family Trauma, Child Custody & Child Development* , Issue 1, pages 2–13.

6. Alexander, Pamela C., 2014, *Intergenerational Cycles of Trauma and Violence: An attachment and family systems perspective*, W. W. Norton & Company.

7. Amos, J., Furber, G. and Segal, L., 2011, 'Understanding maltreating mothers: a synthesis of relational trauma, attachment disorganization, structural dissociation of the personality, and experiential avoidance', *Journal of Trauma Dissociation*. 12(5):495–509.

8. Gershoff, E. T. and Grogan-Kaylor, A., 2016, 'Spanking and child outcomes: Old controversies and new meta-analyses', *Journal of Family Psychology,* Jun;30(4):453–69.

9. Ibid.

10. Bugental, D. B., Lyon, J. E., Lin, E. K., et al., 1999, 'Children "tune out" in response to ambiguous communication style of powerless adults', *Child Development*. 70:214–30.

Chapter 9

1. Eichorn, E. and Huebner, C., 2023, 'Votes at 16 in Scotland': www.sps.ed.ac.uk/sites/default/files/assets/doc/Votes%20at%20 16%20in%20Scotland.pdf

Chapter 10

1. Centers for Disease Control and Prevention, 2021. Youth Risk Behavior Survey Data. Available at: www.cdc.gov/yrbs.

Index